The Guinea Pig
In the Freezer

Life, Laughter, and a
Little Miracle

JOEL VERNIER

"Comfy Chair" publishing

ISBN:1539629333
ISBN-13:9781539629337

DEDICATION

I dedicate this book to my daughter Chris and to all of the animals that have enriched our lives. To all parents who have, will, or are raising children and to everyone that enjoys a little humor.

CONTENTS

ACKNOWLEDGMENTS

My deepest thanks to all of my friends, family and acquaintances that have heard me tell these stories, enjoyed them, and encouraged me to write this book to share with everyone.

Special thanks to: my Mom & Dad who always taught me to do the right thing in life, and to my brother Larry who showed me how to live that philosophy with his life. Thanks to Chelsea Cleary who provided the artwork for this book, and who will have an amazing future as an artist. To Terri Kennedy for photo of Blossom & Woodrow . To Theresa Ekdom who had the patience to walk me through the editing and publishing process. Thanks to the medical team that helped me get into remission, and to my faith in God that has sustained me.

"Remember, every day is a gift! Some are just a little more fun to open than others"

~ Joel

PREFACE

This book is dedicated to people who enjoy looking at life with a smile. Life is a great adventure; it has a beginning and an end. The beginning is full of promise; the end needs to be a fulfillment of that promise.

For new parents, or parents-to-be, this may offer some insight into the journey that is ahead of you. For experienced parents, this may trigger some of your own memories and stories. For people who have not had children, it may give you some insights into the episodic insanity that occurs periodically when parenting.

When my life was first blessed with my daughter Christina, people asked, "Did having a baby affect your lifestyle?" The answer is, "No, it didn't affect my life style. It eliminated my lifestyle and I grew a new one!"

My new lifestyle indeed was an enriched life with new experiences, delights, wonders, surprises, shocks, and heartbreaks. Having a child, a new life to help nurture, grow, develop into a unique individual has been the most meaningful and truly enjoyable focus of my life!

My daughter Christina, like many children changed her name as she continued to mature: Christina, Chrissy and end up as Chris! "A rose by any other name…" Shakespeare. He must have raised a child or observed one growing up.

Some of you have transitioned from the city to the country, or the country to the city. I hope there will be some memories that will bring a smile to your hearts.

For the many people who have dealt with illness, or who are dealing with illness, my heart goes out to you. I offer you this: Remember that every day is a gift; some are just a little more fun to open than others!

I have shared various stories of this adventure with friends and family. Several of them said, "You need to write a book and share these stories with the world."

Well, here it goes…

1 THE NEW BEGINNING

I came home from work one brisk February evening, and was greeted by my Golden Retriever, Penny. For the benefit of those who don't know the breed, they've been bred to blend well into the company of humans.

Golden Retrievers are a smart breed; friendly and, in my opinion, quite beautiful. With that said, the Golden is a socially needy dog. They're so much fun to have around, as they're constantly instigating some activity that they want to draw you into. Some Goldens will carry around a toy, a ball, your sock or any object that they can mouth, bringing it to you to show you their treasure. They'll parade around you and tease you, trying to get you to take the object away and to reward them with petting or a treat, or to go outside and to play with them. Penny was trained to retrieve about 35 different items and knew each one by name.

Between retrieving items, walks, fetch, grooming and snuggling, you can pretty much spend your entire life trying to satiate your Golden. This, indeed, was Penny's goal.

In order to reach Penny's satiation point, you'd have to pet her 24/7 until your arm shriveled up and blew away. Essentially, there is no satiation point, that's the real deal.

1

But the fact is, they are a warm, wonderful addition to any family.

On a cold night, one can enjoy the 103.5 F given off by the family pooch. Of course the bigger the dog, the more heat they can share with you. I just love sitting on the couch with one of my favorite blankets, with my dog lying next to me. Central Michigan can at times feel like the Arctic Circle.

∽

Now, on a normal bone-chilling Michigan evening, my wife Carol would be busy in the kitchen whipping up some tasty recipe for dinner. The TV would be blaring, the fireplace blazing.

In Michigan on a cold February night, this is a welcomed additional source of warmth. But not on this night! The lights were on, but no TV blared forth, no fire produced heat, and there was no dinner filling the house with aromatic anticipation!

The Vernier family is a bit food-focused; in fact, my relatives have had more gastric bypasses than most families have had tonsils out, so this was a noted concern. No dinner? Quieting my hunger pangs a little, I began to look for Carol. First I looked in the kitchen, but I did not find her there. So where should I look? Oh, the bathroom, of course! There was Carol, holding something in her hand.

She looked at me and said, "The rabbit died!"

Well, since we didn't have a rabbit at this point in our lives, it could only mean one thing… a baby!

For the younger generation, in the olden days, (and yes, I seem to be referring to the olden days more often than not, now that I am older;) a physician would obtain a urine sample from a woman and inject it into a live rabbit. If she was pregnant, it would cause bulging masses on the ovaries of the rabbit. The rabbit was killed in order to see if the masses were, indeed present. If they were, the woman was determined to be pregnant, hence the saying, "The rabbit died." A good reference article is "The Rabbit Died," by Robin Elise Weiss.

I was so excited at the thought of having a baby! We had wondered if God would ever bless us with a child, since we had been trying for several years.

We'd decided that going to a fertility doctor was a good thing for many people to try, (except possibly "Octo-mom, wow 8 babies") but for us, we would leave it in God's hands. Wow, what a gift we received!

The excitement of a baby creates many changes as an individual, and even more changes as a couple. It must be part of God's master plan to prepare you for the oncoming onslaught of commitment and lifestyle changes. Let the episodic insanity begin!

The next nine months seemed to fly by; we were busy making the preparations that all parents, particularly first-time parents, do. The baby's room; the baby furniture; the baby clothes; the baby toys (I had a tendency to get carried away with the toy part). As an example, when Christina was about six, some new friends came over, looked around the house and asked, "How many children do you have?"

"Just one," I sheepishly replied.

I thought to myself at the time that it was a good thing that we kept most of her toys in an extra bedroom, otherwise people might get the idea that I spoil my daughter.

While the nine months flew by for me, Carol might take exception to time's passage. Carol, after all, was the one who went through the metamorphosis from a normal, healthy woman to a normal, healthy pregnant woman.

And as for the dad-to-be, I observed the morning sickness, the physical changes, (I gained some weight!) and exhibited some of the mental impact of pregnancy. Carol indeed had various food cravings, and emotional states, and so did I.

And like all women in that delicate condition, Carol glowed! Indeed, we went through the Lamaze classes and yes, I did get the breathing and panting thing down. We attended the parenting classes. But nothing, and I mean nothing, can prepare you for the actual event.

Planning for the event, I felt like I was preparing for the Manhattan Project: Fat Man and Little Boy had nothing on us! All the data was reviewed, all the scenarios discussed, but nothing could have prepared them for the real thing.

When the actual explosion went off, when the blinding brilliance lit up the sky, when the shock wave overcame them... Wow! Reality is so real! And so is childbirth.

The night was October 2, 1990. The days building up to my daughter's birth created a sense of heightened excitement, a nervous energy, and a breathless anticipation. Oh, heck! I was nearly out of my mind with the waiting. Every time Carol had a contraction I was heading for the phone and ready to drive her to the hospital.

She'd slow me down. "Cool your jets," she'd say, "It's not time yet!"

How did she know? I must've drifted off during that teaching moment in the parenting class.

I decided I should go to bed and get some sleep. I lay down, said my prayers and drifted off to sleep.

The next thing I knew, Carol woke me up and said, "It's time to go to the hospital!"

Wow, what an adrenalin rush! The Manhattan Project; the moment that a hunter places his sights on a beautiful 10-point buck; hooking a sailfish on an ocean charter; winning the lottery; the space shuttle take off! All these emotions seemed to ignite my neurons.

I watched Carol have one of the contractions; this was no little contraction, but a world-class contraction. All I could think of was a Roadrunner cartoon.

You know the one where Wiley Coyote has a bottle of ACME Earthquake Pills? He accidentally swallows some pills and he has an earthquake in his body.

It starts as a little tremor in his finger and builds to a shaking tremor of his whole body. This is what Carol's contractions looked like.

Of course, you don't just GO to the hospital. You have to call and let them know that you're coming, as if they wouldn't know when you got there. You need to make sure that the overnight bag is in the car; you need to make sure your wife is in the car. Then you have to drive to the hospital.

Wow! What a drive! Every time Carol had a Wiley Coyote Earthquake Contraction, she would grab my hand, squeezing it tightly. And, of course, my speed would increase.

On the I-75 expressway, I'd be driving 70 mph, then as she squeezed my hand, 75 . . . 80 . . . 85 . . . and 90! The contraction would subside and I would notice my speed and slow back down.

You should know that I always drive the speed limit. "Safety first" is a motto that I live by. But this was a special night, and I was having an "out of my mind" experience. Thank God that it was late at night; almost no traffic. It took only 20 minutes to get to the hospital, but it seemed to take forever.

I pulled up to the emergency entrance, stopped the car and ran for a wheelchair. I rolled Carol up to the admitting nurse.

She asked, "Is this your first baby?"

Carol said, "Yes it is."

Then the nurse told us, "Oh, don't worry, you're in for a long night. First babies take their time."

Well, I couldn't take the suspense any longer. In situations like this, it seems that I inherited my grandmother Josephine's intuitive thinking.

Josephine was a true artist; an accomplished painter and writer who had a touch of ESP. Some call it a psychic power; I prefer intuitive thinking. Whatever it is, I have, on occasion, had premonitions about future or real-time events that have proven correct and had a positive effect on certain outcomes.

As an example: in college, I went camping with a couple of high school buddies at Bald Mountain Campground in Lake Orion, Michigan. It was a calm night, and we went to sleep about 11:30 p.m. Later, I woke up in a sweat, with one thought: we had to leave, immediately! I didn't know why, but I knew we had to leave. One buddy said to go back to sleep. My other friend looked at me, observed my intensity and sweat and said, "If Joel says we have to go, let's go!" We packed up and headed for home.

When we arrived home, we turned on the TV for the morning news, and, unbelievable as it sounds, a tornado had hit the Bald Mountain Campgrounds not long after we left! So, I've come to trust my intuition.

I yelled at the nurse. "You have to take her in immediately; she's dilated to 5 centimeters!"

The nurse gave me a strange look, but decided to take Carol back immediately. After what seemed to be an eternity, the nurse came back and said, "She IS dilated to 5 centimeters. How could you possibly have known that? Hurry and park your car and we'll get you into the birthing room with your wife!"

I hurried up, parked the car and ran back to the hospital. The nurse ushered me into the room, where Carol was focused on the task at hand, to say the least.

As a male, I will never know the sensation of giving birth, and that may be by the Creator's design!

I know that some women have a very easy time of it, and that others have suggested that it would be like peeing out a bowling ball, you know, like passing a kidney stone. A Hebrew saying states that God knew He couldn't be everywhere, and that's why He created mothers. God bless all mothers, past, present and future; without you, we wouldn't be here today.

Birthing was reality, and Carol was having a tough go at it. I tried talking to her, sharing the instructions we learned at Lamaze classes and her comments to me sounded a lot like something a burly street fighter might come up with in a dark alley when asking for your wallet.

The nurses told me this was completely normal; unfortunately, I didn't have a dictionary to look up some of the utterances, although they might not have even been in the dictionary.

Suddenly, Carol's water broke, and the head nurse said, "We have meconium in the amniotic fluid, get her husband out of here!"

The nurses ushered me out and said to wait in the hallway. I had no idea what was going on, but I waited and let the professionals do their thing. Later, I learned that it meant the baby had a bowel movement in the amniotic fluid. This could cause an infection and put the baby at risk. Fortunately, there was no infection. Amen!

After what seemed to be forever, the nurses called me back in and told me that everything was all right. They went on to explain that the OBGYN had performed an episiotomy on Carol to help the birthing process.

What is it about the medical profession that it has to come up with big complicated words for everything they talk about and everything they do? An episiotomy is a small incision to increase the size of the birth opening. Ok, then, just say that. But no, they have to call it an episiotomy.

Then, it happened. The miracle of life that has been repeated time after time, since Adam and Eve had their first child. Kings, paupers and slaves, all of humanity has the blessing of this gift. Yes, I witnessed the miracle of Carol giving birth to our daughter: I felt exhausted.

The OBGYN asked me if I wanted to cut the umbilical cord. I quickly replied that I didn't want to participate in that aspect of childbirth and that he was being sufficiently paid to cut the cord. Really, I felt squeamish about it, and concerned that I might make a mistake. "Safety first", remember!

As all parents do, we agonized over and role-played almost all of the names in several books that we bought on the subject.

We started with the A's, and went progressively to the Z's. As we spoke the names out loud over a period of months, we played rhyme games with them, made playground bastardization of the names and attempted to come up with an acceptable list. Also, we found that what sounded good one day, didn't feel right the next day. We were at our wits' end over the name game. Then one day, I thought about the world we live in. The world today is fraught with challenges, frustrations, dangers and temptations.

The name Christina kept surfacing through the haze of names floating around in my head. Christina: it has a nice sound. It's formal, and yet feminine. The name has Christ in it; this may have some benefits as she grows up and moves out into the world.

Christina is a Greek name, derived from "royalty." She could be called Chris, or Chrissy, or Tina. The middle name Marie just seemed to go with Christina. And it was agreed upon that our daughter would be called Christina Marie Vernier.

So there we were, in a birthing room at Pontiac General Hospital, in Pontiac, Michigan. The room was furnished with Mom's bed in the front of the room, and a very comfortable rocking chair in the back.

I sat down in the rocker; the nurse brought my beautiful Christina and handed her to me.

What a feeling! I was overcome by warm, glowing thoughts of what an incredible little miracle I held in my hands. Parental emotions flowed through me like a mighty river. In a Gestalt moment, I felt the awesome responsibility, the absolute wonder, the future concerns and worries that are inevitable. Ah, yes, it truly was a Kodak moment. Of course, the camera was at home, and camera phones weren't invented yet.

While rocking back and forth, cradling my new baby, I felt the need to communicate with my daughter.

I spoke softly, introducing myself to her; telling her of all the experiences that lay in front of her. I told her where she would live, and about Penny, our dog. Then it happened - out of nowhere, a little song came to mind.

Sweet pea, sweet pea, Daddy loves his little sweet pea. Sweet pea, sweet pea, Daddy loves his little girl!"

Big emotions of pure love welled up inside of me, and tears ran down my cheeks. Little did I know that I would keep singing that song to her, every night, to this day.

Carol and Christina spent the next two and a half days at the hospital. I was there most of the time, except to go home, take care of our Penny and get some sleep. Our families came to visit. It was such an exciting time! Everyone was so happy to see Christina and Mom.

∾

One aspect of our society has always puzzled me: everyone loves babies, and generally seems very tolerant of them. Why is it, then, as babies grow up, become teenagers and then adults, that we as a society become less tolerant? Is it the pure innocence and helplessness that makes us smile? As people turn into adults, do we value them less? I've often wondered about this social moray.

I guess it's similar with puppies, kittens and bunnies; they're so cute when they're little, but as they grow up, they lose their cuteness, and get less time devoted to them.

It must be in God's great plan that babies of all species are advantaged by the cuteness factor, to help them by eliciting such fondness from adults. That might not be true for snakes and spiders, but for most critters it rings true!

∾

Then came time for the ride home.

Carol was still in quite a bit of pain from the episiotomy, and she felt every bump in the road. I drove as carefully as I could and tried to miss the potholes and road cracks that are always present in the colder northern climates.

Basically, there are three driving seasons in Michigan: Winter, Under Construction, and Heading Up North on a Friday! Up North is a tradition in Michigan, for throngs of people who've worked all week and need to take a pilgrimage to the north country to de-stress and relax.

I finally pulled up to our home on Fawn Valley with Carol and Christina. Out on the lawn was a large stork statue. It included all of the pertinent birth information, including date, length and weight.

I always wondered why the length and weight were so important. It's not like fishing. If the baby isn't long enough or heavy enough, you really can't throw them back, right?

Our home had recently gone through restoration. Yes, a complete childproofing, baby-accommodating restoration. We put childproof locks on all of the cupboards; we moved all the breakables out of reach. We plugged all of the unplugged outlets. We blocked the entrances to the stairways and put safety locks on the doors. We threw out old medications, hid the liquor, and cleaned the refrigerator.

We had brand new baby furniture, baby towels, baby clothing, baby car seat, baby mobiles, baby stuffed animals, baby noise makers, baby chairs, baby food and baby toys. We had baby videos, baby formula, baby blankets, baby books, and baby diapers – yes, disposable. There is a landfill in the Clarkston area that should have been named after my daughter.

At this point, I could barely see myself changing a diaper, let alone using a cloth diaper and scraping it out. Actually, it wasn't long until changing a diaper would be no big deal, but I preferred the disposables.

We entered the house and went directly into the family room. As we passed the dining room, I noticed that the dining room table was stacked to the ceiling with all types of baby paraphernalia.

It reminded me of a scene from the movie "Turner and Hooch." Turner stopped at the grocery store to pick up a few things, mentioned to the store clerk that he needed some doggie items to stop the dog from chewing, etc. The clerk loaded up the cart with a zillion doggie items and at the checkout, Turner made a big scene about the cost of the items.

Now, according to the Consumer Expenditure Survey by the U.S. Department of Labor, conducted from 1990-92, (the figures have been updated to 2001 dollars using the Consumer Price Index), the cost of raising a child to 17 is approximately $124, 800 dollars. Hey, Turner, Hooch is a bargain!

This would be our first night as a complete family. We had dinner, of course, while learning a new skill set; taking turns eating dinner and smothering Christina with love and affection. We had the television on, with the volume turned low.

Carol took care of the diaper changes and, of course, the feedings, on our first day home.

This would soon change. About 9:00 p.m. Carol said she was exhausted and wanted to go to bed for a while, and that she would get up in a couple of hours to take a turn watching the baby. I was ok with that. I held Christina in my arms and I sang her the "Sweet Pea" song and just relaxed on the couch.

As time went by, I realized that I hadn't been taught how to lay the baby down in her bassinet. In fact, I really didn't know much, other than how to hold her. This could be a long night!

By 1:00 a.m. I was exhausted. I quietly yelled (I know,) up to Carol, who was in deep sleep in the upstairs master bedroom, but to no avail. Carol is a gifted sleeper; she has the ability to sleep through most common noises, phone calls, people trying to wake her up, sonic booms and tactical nukes going off. To say that she's a sound sleeper does not truly explain her gift.

And then it happened: I fell asleep with baby in my arms. Carol came down about 7:00 a.m. and woke me. Believe it or not, I was sleeping all night and was still cradling Christina in my arms. I know it was a stupid thing to do, but this is another example of episodic insanity.

∽

When you bring home a new baby, and you have a Golden Retriever who's used to being the center of attention and is now downgraded in the pecking order, there may be some issues to deal with.

We attempted to circumvent these issues by taking the following steps: I brought home Christina's sleepwear from the hospital and let Penny smell it. I also placed it in Penney's bed to acclimate her to the scent.

When we brought Christina home, we introduced her to Penny. We let Penny smell her and lick her. We petted Penny and talked to her, with lots of positive soft words to make her feel good about the transition. The important issue to keep in mind, when you have a pet in your home, is that an animal is an animal. Animals can change behavior in an instant.

This is a true fact of life. Overall, having Christina at home seemed to be a positive experience for Penny. However, one incident occurred when Christina was beginning to walk. She stumbled, as all babies do when learning to walk, and fell down on Penny. Penny let out a low, deep, and ominous growl!

I moved swiftly, picked up Christina and handed her to Mom. Then at lightning speed, I grabbed Penny, turned her on her back, (a submissive position) and loudly scolded her.

I guess it was a rather intense scolding. Carol said that the voice that emerged from me sounded a lot like Mercedes Cambridge's interpretation of the demonic Satan voice from the movie "The Exorcist." I'm sure the "Dog Whisperer" Cesar Milan wouldn't have approved, but the fact is, it worked.

There was never another incident, even when Christina would bump into or fall on Penny. In the future, all was well. Thank God! Christina and Penny became fast friends. They played together, snuggled together, and yes, at times, even ate together. Christina, unfortunately, developed a taste for dog food and treats that she later outgrew.

This magic relationship between a child and a dog would be repeated twice later in her life with Snowy and Chloe. There are tales of unbelievable devotion and love.

∽

As with all new babies, family and friends are exceedingly generous and helpful.

We took up my in-laws on their offer to come over and stay to help us get used to our new life. We were very grateful for their help.

The next few months moved slowly. The term "caregiver" really applies to this period in child development. There are feedings, changings, more feedings and more changings. There are holding times, rocking times, crying times, bathing times, more feeding times, changing times, laughing times, giggling times, smiling times, chuckling times, some scary times, and did I mention the feeding times?

The scary times are when baby is not feeling well. Temperature is up, the face is red, and the disposition is unhappy. Then, the parents aren't feeling well either.

For me, these were very difficult times. When a baby is so little and helpless, you want to do everything in your power to keep baby safe, warm, happy, and fed.

The problem is, at this age, your child cannot talk. You can't ask them what's wrong, or where they hurt. I had a very difficult time with this.

I'm sure our pediatrician really became tired of hearing from me.

Especially on the weekends, which is, oddly enough, the times that Christina usually became ill. "Safety first," of course, so I would call our pediatrician at the first sign of discomfort.

Interesting, isn't it, that veterinarians and pediatricians have to be highly talented diagnosticians. They both are caregivers to patients who can't tell them what's wrong or what's hurting them.

To Christina's pediatrician: Thank you for putting up with me through those years, and God bless you!

Granted, babies can communicate with us through a variety of non-verbal ways. To me, the most direct link was to gaze in Christina's eyes.

It's been said that the eyes are the windows to the soul. When I looked into my daughter's eyes, I felt a direct link into her soul, her developing mind and being. Our time together during those years was very rewarding. We would go on walks; the stroller was put to good use. We would go to church on Sunday morning and often we would play together.

This practice continued through Christina's later years. We would call them Daddy/Daughter dates. Of course, later in the teen years I remember them more as shopping sprees!

I truly loved the early development years. Each of the stages that children go through elicited new and exciting activities, videos and pictures.

And, I took great pleasure in buying her new toys and stuffed animals to play with.

One of the surprises of being a new Daddy was the glow of self-fulfillment that care giving generates. All children are dependent on Mommy and Daddy in the early years for everything. It's an awesome responsibility, and an awesome gift from God to have and enjoy these times.

It also seems that, in our children's eyes, we go through many changes as parents.

At first, we know absolutely everything. Then, we know some things; then we know absolutely nothing! As our children get older, at some point they realize that we didn't know everything, but we did know some things. And then we begin to forget things and they begin to help the parents. The circle of life.

∾

Baby and toddler clothing should be rented, not bought. Having an only child should be grounds for financial aid. I was amazed at how clothing would never wear out. There was no time, they were simply outgrown.

Mothers, grandmothers, friends and aunts love going shopping. But it seems they're mesmerized with shopping for baby and toddler clothes.

When they're at the store, they'll pick up a clothing item, then they squeal with joy as they discuss how cute the item is. They talk about when to wear the item, how much fun the little girl will have wearing the item, how much fun it is shopping for baby and toddler items. Then they set it down and go on to the next item!

I truly think that they go back in time and space, just while shopping, to when they were little girls playing with their dolls. It's the only way I can explain their behavior.

The good news is, they do end up purchasing lots and lots of clothing items that may only last a couple of months. The items then are off to younger siblings or to friends who have children a little younger, for their use.

∾

One very important issue for parents is that childrearing can become so all-encompassing, and you can lose yourself so completely, that your relationship may suffer. It's so important to enrich the magic of growing up, that the magic of the relationship can be placed on hold.

Take the time. Couples need to spend some "Me time" with each other. Continue to do the little things that will grow your relationship. Go out to dinner, a show, or just spend some private time together.

A loving relationship between mom and dad, or, for single parents, remaining happy with your own life, is critical for your children's growth and development.

Divorce can be devastating for children. Staying in a sour relationship can also be devastating. Be vigilant, be happy, and stay loving, or have the courage to end an unhealthy relationship.

Being human isn't easy, but it is human.

2 FIRST AND NEXT YEARS

The first year is full of so many, well, firsts. We began calling Christina 'Chrissy'.

Chrissy's first Christmas; what joy! Everything seemed fresh and new for Carol and me, including decorating the house, and all of the holiday preparations. This included leaving milk and cookies for Santa, apples for his reindeer and, of course, the Christmas presents! And to me, that means toys!

Chrissy received many presents. Presents from my side of the family and Carol's side; from friends, Mom, Dad, and the jolly man himself, Santa Claus. This was the beginning of Chrissy's love of Christmas and her love of presents.

Chrissy was only 3 months old on her first Christmas. She did need a little help opening her presents. Talk about growing quickly - some of the beautiful clothing gifts were outgrown by the time they were opened at Christmas!

Some families open presents on Christmas Eve. When I was younger, that puzzled me, because Santa hadn't had the chance to come and leave the presents yet.

Some families open presents on Christmas morning, the more traditional time.

Our family participated in both traditions. Christmas Eve was for our relatives' gifts at my Mom and Dad's. This was followed by Christmas morning at our home and Christmas afternoon shared with Carol's side of the family.

By the way, do we really choose sides?

My parents always put on a great buffet at their house, and then, "Let the carnage begin!" The gifts would be exchanged and opened. It always reminded me of sharks participating in a feeding frenzy. Once the first present was opened, the children would get a glazed look in their eyes and the "present frenzy" would begin. This made it tough to take notes on what gift came from whom. We did our best, but sometimes we fell short of keeping up.

∼

Talk about episodic insanity! This time of year, individuals, families - in fact most of the United States - participates in financial suicide. This is enough for Dave Ramsey to turn Grinch Green! Credit cards get maxed, loans are maxed, and bank accounts are emptied, all for the sake of getting presents for the perfect Christmas. In fact, for many retailers, the holiday buying season (to be politically correct) is the difference between solvency and bankruptcy. This is incredible. The reality is that Christmas is already perfect! It was born that way.

I learned a neat lesson, years later from a friend of mine in the Knights of Columbus, a Catholic charity. He was blessed with a child later in life, actually after retirement. We were discussing Christmas preparations.

"How many gifts will your daughter open on Christmas?" I asked.

He paused, looked thoughtful and answered, "Three."

"Only three presents?" I asked. I was wondering how he could possibly get away with such a small number.

"Why three?" I asked for clarification.

"That's what baby Jesus received from the three Wise Men," he answered.

I immediately felt humbled by the blessed logic. Then I thought to myself, where in the world were you when Chrissy was a baby? What a great tradition!

I thought I would pass this on to all new parents of the Christian faith. We all know that the true meaning of Christmas is the celebration of the birth of baby Jesus and the life-changing impact that his life and teachings have made on the world. The presents are just a fun way to celebrate his birthday.

I hadn't learned that lesson, so for most of Chrissy's life, Christmas morning was an overload of presents and the frenzy of opening them. Most of her "Santa List" presents were under the tree.

This is a habit I started with Carol the year before we were engaged. She gave me a list of 24 presents to choose from. Of course, on Christmas I brought all 24 presents, gift wrapped, to her house. It was fun! Her mom said I was a keeper.

As for my gifts, with my intuitive mind, I would usually guess each of my presents correctly. I didn't realize it, but my family hated that. They wanted me to be surprised. So I quit guessing!

At my house we love to watch the TV show "The Mentalist" with Simon Baker. I've intuitively been on target with my guesses so many times that my family takes such things for granted. But they love the show!

Christmas has been, and continues to be, Chrissy's favorite holiday. I nurtured this love of Christmas by bringing home new decorations every year.

For her second Christmas, I brought home a three foot tall plastic Frosty the Snowman. Chrissy adopted "Frosty" as her best friend. We had recently moved into a new neighborhood, and while there were other children in this rather large country subdivision, she hadn't met all of them yet.

So, Frosty had tea parties, watched TV, played with stuffed animals and was dressed up in various outfits. He was indeed a great friend, always ready to play and he never complained! How cute! We still have Frosty, and bring him out each year at Christmas.

When Chrissy was 6, the night came that all parents who celebrate Christmas wish would never come.

Chrissy asked "Daddy is there really a Santa Claus?"

I paused for a moment, and then asked, "Why do you want to know?"

It turned out that the older kids on the school bus gleefully taunted the younger kids, saying that Santa didn't exist.

"Do you want the truth?" I asked.

"Yes!" Chrissy answered.

At that moment, I knew that Chrissy understood the truth, but that she wanted to hear it from me. Then, with a heavy heart, I told her that Santa Claus did not exist as a real live person.

I cried, she cried and Carol cried. Emotions are so much a part of being human. I felt my heart tugging on my soul.

Then, a beautiful thought occurred to me.

I went on to explain that while the Santa Claus, the physical person, did not exist, the "Spirit of Christmas" indeed did exist and can stay alive in everyone, even in their old age, if they choose to believe.

As our discussion continued I gave her a choice: We could move forward now, knowing that there is not a Santa Claus and the "Christmas Magic" will slip away. Or, we could make a decision to continue to live with our imagination, and commit to keeping the "Spirit of Christmas" in our home for years to come.

We would still put out milk and cookies for Santa and apples for his reindeer. There would still be presents under the tree from Santa. We could still decorate the house for Christmas with the same excitement and glee.

Chrissy pondered her choice, thinking about the many ramifications of her decision.

She decided to keep the Christmas Magic in our lives, and it lives on to this day! Every year we decorate the house, put out cookies and milk for Santa, and carrots and apples for his reindeer! What fun!

∾

The firsts continued to accumulate. Chrissy's first New Year's Eve arrived, although she didn't stay up too late for this one.

And then, her first Easter was quickly upon us. Yes, we did the whole 9 yards celebrating this holiday. (Why 9 yards, and not 10 yards?) At night we left out carrots for the Easter Bunny and in the morning, the Easter basket and the hiding of the Easter eggs was ready for Chrissy. And me. I guess I'm just a big kid at heart!

Of course, this first Easter, I hunted and found the eggs as Chrissy observed. I'm not sure who had the most fun!

The Easter egg hunt would become a practice that would evolve into a marathon on future Easter mornings. Hiding the eggs, having Chrissy find them and repeating this act over and over again. Yes, it was fun for all!

Of course, we participated in the mall picture with the Easter Bunny. Why do character suits always seem to have an odor? It was amazing that the candy in the Easter basket disappeared over the next few weeks. In the Vernier family, candy doesn't just disappear; it has a tendency to enhance one's physique. All of the holidays seemed to go by in a whirlwind of renewed excitement and joy.

∾

Like many Michigan residents, we owned a cottage Up North. For those of you who live in other places, in case you are unaware of this fact; for Michiganders, going Up North on a weekend is episodic insanity brought to a new level.

On any given Friday night, it seems the entire Detroit and southern Michigan community participates in a lemming-like trek to get away and go "Up North" to relax and unwind.

Keep in mind, it takes a significant effort to get from Point A: One's Home in The City; to Point B: One's Cottage Up North. The trip Up North is not just a casual drive. It is truly a road-raging, blood-pressure raising, traffic-snarling, wits-ending, "Are we there yet?" It is an awful pilgrimage to Up North!

Once the journey is over, we are called a variety of different names by the locals. "Trunk Slammers"(the noise we make removing luggage from our vehicles); "Fudgies" (we consume massive amounts of a variety of flavors of fudge, most notably from Mackinaw Island); "Citiots" (self-explanatory); Jerky Chompers (we also consume mass quantities of dried meats purchased at gas stations); and "Flatlanders," as southeast Michigan is flat. We also are called "Trolls" by the "Yoopers," the Michiganders from the Upper Peninsula (because we live under the bridge that connects the lower and upper peninsulas of Michigan).

Once we arrive at our northern destination, we then hurry up and relax. Or we at least try to!

Just the expenses incurred going Up North and back, is a costly venture: gasoline, fast food, coffee, aspirin, antihypertensives and stomach antacids. This all translates into a couple of hundred bucks, in transportation.

And, although we are slandered with creative names, we then pour thousands of dollars into the local economies buying what we forgot to bring up. We also spend money on recreational hunting, fishing, boating, trail riding, scenery gawking, book reading, and nap taking. You know - relaxation.

The next thing you know it's Sunday night and it's time for the return pilgrimage home. This is then repeated the very next weekend! We took this journey for 12 years until we moved Up North and became locals ourselves.

Raising a child gives you a chance to watch little miracles in progress. Language development: wonderful sounds, from gurgling, cooing and crying, to recognizing words, saying words, then sentences and conversations. It's a building process that computers, at the time of this writing, can thankfully only mimic.

The development of thinking, creativity, intelligent consciousness and developing emotions is fortunately in the realm of human existence. We also have a beautiful gift from our Creator: our soul.

Mobile-mania is the best way to describe the process of development that occurs when a baby begins sitting - then crawling - at incredible speeds, I might add, it is amazing to see a baby crawl along at such a pace that it's hard to follow. What is it about a baby's ability to crawl and then walk faster than an adult can keep up with? Even well-trained athletes cannot keep pace when they're at home with their children. This is why it is so critical to baby proof a house! Yep, Chrissy was showing her first independence by being mobile.

The march of time is a constant. The only constant in life is change. From the moment we are born, to the moment we die, we are constantly changing. At the cellular level, we are regenerating ourselves and changing every day of our lives.

It's interesting to note that, even though we're immersed in all of these changes, humans resist change. But when does this resistance begin? As we're growing up, we love change. Crawling, standing, walking, running, and getting taller. All of these changes we welcome. We can't wait to get to the next age; 8 ½, 10 ½, but whoever heard of 40 ½?

All of a sudden you are a teenager, getting a license to drive. Then turning 18 and becoming a young adult. Then turning 21, the legal age to enjoy adult beverages in moderation (well, that's what all the ads are telling us to do!). Yes, these changes are good!

At some point we stop welcoming changes. I love this quote from Chili Davis: "Growing old is mandatory. Growing up is optional." Embrace change. Change only ends in this life upon death. The afterlife is another story!

Sometime around her first year, Chrissy said her first word. It happened to be "Da-Da." I was so taken with her first word. I mean, I was thrilled and honored that she chose "Da-Da." If I remember correctly, Carol was less thrilled. After all, Carol usually spent the most time with Chrissy, and worked the hardest taking care of her. Yes, there may have been a little good-hearted jealousy that she said "Da-Da" first. I attributed it to the fact that I was not with her as much, due to working and traveling. Indeed, her next word was "Muh-Muh." Carol was thrilled.

And in the blink of an eye, we were celebrating her second birthday! Of course we had a birthday party with all the relatives, and presents, and "Rosco the Clown." I'm sure every community has a local clown that does kid's parties, with balloon animals and old jokes. The kids loved him! He was tall and an older clown, but he delivered his jokes with good humor.

Carol and I had a rather large outdoor play set built, with a fort, slides, and swings. My dad was very unhappy when he saw her climb up the ladder to the fort and then down the slide she would go! He was concerned that she might fall climbing the ladder. Dad was at times overprotective, but he meant well.

Even at an early age, Chrissy was developing into an athletic little girl. I assured Grandpa that it was ok and playtime continued. She loved her play set and enjoyed countless hours playing with her friends.

I remember her first complete sentence. It was early evening and we were playing in the family room. You know, the innocent tickle play? I had invented the

"Claw" I would raise my hand up and the "Claw" would attack and tickle. I would usually embellish with a comment, "The Claw is hungry, and it wants to eat you!" The giggles were well worth the efforts!

Then Chrissy walked over to the sliding glass door, ran her hand along the door, not looking at me, and she said, "Daddy, I love you!"

Wow, what welling up of emotions! I felt like Martin Short in the movie "Pure Luck" when a bee stung him. He swelled up hugely! That's how I felt inside; so filled up with feelings I thought I might explode.

I felt so proud, humbled, joyous, ecstatic; you know, a warm and fuzzy feeling all over. Wow! I ran over and picked her up and said, "I love you too, Chrissy!"

∾

I don't know who invented this particular tool that is called a variety of names; pacifier, binky, num-num. Well whatever it is called there is no doubt for some children it has a calming effect and it keeps them quiet. I was not thrilled that we used this tool, but we did use it.

This was an addiction in the truest of sense. I remember one night when we trekked up north. It was dark, rainy and foggy. When we arrived, we discovered something inconceivable - no binky!

When Chrissy realized that her binky was nowhere to be found, she became very vocal. Needless to say, I ended up taking a one-hour drive up to the next town that had a K-Mart, and I bought three binkies.

What a night! Our cottage is located in Mid-Michigan, in an area that is not well-lit. When driving, particularly at night, you have to be very careful. You have to watch out for other cars, and Amish buggies! The Amish buggies are tough to see at night, as the lights are quite dim. Then you have to watch for deer, bears, and a myriad of small animals that might cross the road. And on this night, thick, pea soup fog! It took an hour and a half, but I returned home, the Hero of the Binky!

I spent some time reading and asking pediatricians what is the best method of de-binky-ing a child. I was told cold turkey was the best method; it just seemed cruel. I was told to wean her off the binky, reduce binky time each day, but it seemed too complicated. So the binky addiction continued.

Then one day we were shopping together and Chrissy wanted two different toys. I told her she had to choose, after all we have a budget and it limited her to only one toy. She had to choose between a battery powered kitty, or a toy ball. She chose the ball.

When we arrived at home, Chrissy was not happy. I could see was bothered as we drove back home. She had really liked the kitty and when we were at home, she asked if I would get her the kitty. I then had an epiphany, an A-Ha! moment.

"Chrissy, I know you really want the kitty toy. I'll make a deal with you: you give me all your binkies. You will have to give up your binkies forever, and I'll return to K-Mart and buy you the kitty toy."

"You will, really?" Chrissy asked.

I quickly replied, "Yes, I will, but no more binkies. Do we have a deal?"

She thought for a moment and said "Ok, but on one condition; that you take all my binkies to K-Mart, sell them and put the money toward my toy. It will help with our budget."

"Deal," I said.

Now, as it turns out, the market for used binkies is quite limited, but I did take her binkies back to K-Mart and gleefully threw them in the trash inside the store. I then purchased her kitty toy and returned home.

Chrissy was delighted with her toy, and then unexpectedly asked if I sold her binkies.

I was taken aback for a moment, then responded, "The binkies are at K-Mart right now."

She was happy with my response, and the binky days were at an end!

As Chrissy continued to grow and develop, like all children, she asked a zillion questions. Some parents respond very minimally to such questions. I have heard some respond saying, "Shut up! Can't you see I'm watching the television?" Others give a quick answer: "Because God made it that way." Other parents answer the question, and the child is satisfied.

Well, unfortunately for Chrissy, she would ask me a question and I would answer it in great detail. An example might be "Daddy, were does electricity come from?" I guess I viewed this as a teaching moment. I would begin with a discussion on how electricity is generated, focusing in on coal, gas, hydroelectric, nuclear energy, and wind as some of the ways electricity was generated.

We discussed the next step, how electricity is conducted through high-tension power lines, and the electric power is brought into our home via underground wires to the plugs. We discussed the wonders of electricity and of course, my "Safety First" lecture on the dangers of electricity.

Carol would give me The Look. You know, The Look! Then she would shake her head and say something like "Joel, can't you just keep it simple?" Then she would walk away.

Chrissy never seemed to mind. I asked her years later if she remembered the in depth way that I answered the questions and she said "Yes, I appreciated that you were complete in your answers, and that you kept them on a level I could understand."

You do need to be aware of the perspective of their questions. We've all heard of the story of the child asking her mother, "What is sex?" The mother, with some embarrassment, then goes into the full-blown explanation, and then asks, "Why do you want to know?" The child replies that she is filling out a form for a toy gift from a cereal box and that the form asked for the name, age and sex.

Yes, I believe that if she was ever on a TV show like "Millionaire" or "Cash Cab" that I would be her "phone a friend" or "telephone shout out!"

∽

We have all heard of the "Terrible Twos." This is a label put on children who are testing out their independence and trying to learn their boundaries.

Indeed, when high energy is transformed into physical action, spiced with pushing the limits of a parent's patience, a recipe for emotional outbursts is simmering in the pot.

I remember a time when we were in a Kroger store shopping for groceries and Chrissy wanted a food item. It seemed a reasonable request. Then down the next aisle she wanted another item, but I said no. Well, Chrissy decided that this would be a great time to push the limits a little and obtain the item she wanted from the store.

She began with a low level temper-tantrum.

I asked her to change her behavior, that her behavior was not appropriate. My calmness escalated her energy into a full-blown, red-faced, tear streaming, voice-screaming feet kicking, arm flailing, red alert! It was an I'm a gonna get my way temper tantrum!

Now, keep in mind, my shopping cart was half full with groceries. I asked Chrissy to stop, or else we would leave; to no avail, of course. Once the meltdown reaches a certain level, putting in the rods has no effect.

So, in one gentle swoop I picked Chrissy up in my arms, left the shopping cart half full and we left the store, purchasing nothing.

On the drive home, Chrissy calmed down and said she was sorry. I accepted her apology, but stood my ground and we went home. I hoped that this would be a lesson learned. And it was!

Correcting Chrissy to elicit a change in behavior was not accomplished with hitting or spanking. I would issue a concern or warning that if the behavior continued it would result in the loss of a privilege. It was a great learning curve for father and daughter.

A punishment might include loss of TV time, loss of an electronic game, loss of a favorite treat, or loss of a favorite activity for a period of time. I remember one time that Chrissy lost her Sega game for a week. She noticed that I wasn't happy punishing her.

She asked, "Daddy, are you mad at me?"

I replied, "No, I'm just sorry that you're losing this privilege. I know how much you enjoy playing Sega."

"You mean you don't like punishing me?" she asked.

"No, I don't, but I need to help you learn appropriate behavior, so you will grow up correctly."

Chrissy understood, and even though she tried to negotiate a shorter grounding period, she knew my motivation was to help her. Being consistent and reasonable with privilege-based punishments seemed to keep a proper balance in our family.

Chrissy and I continued to develop a strong bond of love. That beautiful Daddy-Daughter relationship was a true gift! It started when she was very young.

One night I was having a nightmare; a really bad dream. I was with Chrissy in the dream, and a dark evil monster was chasing us. The monster had no discernible shape. The dream was in color; a dark reddish hue. The monster seemed insatiable, and unstoppable. It kept coming for us, and it was a very dark beyond red.

All of a sudden, I awoke to hear Chrissy screaming from her bedroom. I ran to her.

She said, "Dad you had the same dream as me! Thanks for not letting the monster get me. I love you daddy!"

"I love you, too, Chrissy." That is a true story. Wow, what a night.

For the first three years of Chrissy's life, Carol worked as a computer programmer. She would pack up our daughter and drive her 30 minutes to Grandma and Grandpa's.

We felt so fortunate to have them as caregivers for Chrissy. At first the drive wasn't too bad. Some babies sleep pretty well in a car. So Carol would take Chrissy on her way to work and I'd pick her up and take her home. As Chrissy got older, she really came to dislike the car ride. I would play games with her to make it interesting.

As we drove along the expressway and came upon a bridge over the road, I'd say "Duck!" and we would lower our heads and duck until we passed the bridge.

As she became more advanced we played "I Spy." One of us would describe a color or a shape, and then the other would have to guess what the opponent was looking at. The game moved fast because we were moving at 70 miles an hour, so we had to guess quickly.

In addition to the transit from Grandpa and Grandma's, we also had the weekly drive Up North! Our solution was a full size Ford Conversion Van with a TV, video player and connections for the Sega game. We could make the trek Up North in about one and a half movies.

Preschool was suddenly upon us. Carol quit work to be a full-time care giver. Chrissy really loved going to pre-school, especially the days that Carol worked as a teacher's assistant. Carol also loved working there. I was delighted with Chrissy's socialization progress.

The only challenge we found with pre-school was, of course, the viruses that Chrissy caught. It seemed as though every other week she came home with something: flu, pink eye, fever, a rash or a cold. All a part of immunity building.

And then the big step up to Kindergarten. Wow! This first day was so important. I arranged my schedule to go with Carol and drive her to her first day of school! The buildup to this moment had an electrifying, high-energy feel as we ramped up to this historic event!

We took Chrissy to school, and as we walked her up to the building, she seemed a little tenuous. I also felt some ambivalence; I knew that she was growing up!

I asked, "Are you doing ok?"

She said she was, but wanted to know when we were going to pick her up.

I told her, "When you get out of school, we will be here!"

I learned to be very careful when speaking to children; they listen within their own framework. I had learned this earlier in my life when my best friend's son all of a sudden became deathly afraid of Santa. He had always loved Santa, but this particular year wanted nothing to do with him.

In fact, when visiting Santa at the mall, (now, exactly why do character suits have an odor?) he refused to sit in Santa's lap. Over several days, his mom tried to understand what he was afraid of. As it turned out, he had listened to a Christmas song on the radio and what he heard was, that "Santa 'ate' tiny reindeer!" Of course the lyric is, "Santa has eight tiny reindeer." It certainly made "child sense" logic.

Another lesson is that anytime you suggest, hint, or state that you will do something for the child, such as a reward, before you realize it you have entered into an iron-clad, rock-solid, in concrete, no lawyer can get you out of, legally binding contract simply called "You said!" Indeed, words have meaning!

Well the day went by, Chrissy was supposed to be out of school at 3:15 pm. At 2:45 Carol and I were at the school because we couldn't wait to see our daughter and ask her how much she enjoyed her first day. As we sat in the parking lot we noticed a lot of commotion in the school hallways. Several people were running around. Then all of a sudden, coming around the corner of the school building was, and I couldn't believe my eyes, Chrissy!

I yelled, "Carol, look!"

We flung open the car doors and ran over to Chrissy. When she saw us she started crying and ran toward us.

After we embraced and calmed her down, we asked her what was she doing walking around outside the school?

"You said (the binding contract) you'd be here to meet me when I got out of school. Where've you been?" she cried.

Wow! It certainly made "child sense." We explained to her that we meant school ended at 3:15 and we would be here when school ended and the teachers released them from class.

Oh gosh, the teachers. I remembered the commotion in the hallways. We walked Chrissy back into school and her teacher came running over, calling out, "Chrissy, where have you been?"

We explained the situation to her teacher who was relieved. She had alerted the staff - that was the commotion we observed - but now all was well.

It turns out that Chrissy had simply decided that her school day was indeed over. She got up and walked out of class, down the hall and out of the building. When she didn't see us, she walked around the building looking for us.

We gained an agreement with Chrissy that she would wait until classes ended and the teacher released her before she left the classroom.

∾

Winters in Michigan are beautiful. There's nothing like the serenity of a fresh snowfall under a bright blue sky. I love the sound of giggling children playing in the snow, making snow angels, or a snowman.

You can hear the rumbling hum of snowmobiles off in the distance. The chugging of snow blowers and of course, the sirens of ambulances picking up heart attack victims who wanted to save money and shovel snow by hand! The victims are usually male. Why is that? We have more heart attacks and we statistically die younger than women. Not fair!

One beautiful day with fresh snow, Chrissy wanted to go sledding with the neighbors and their children. Carol had told me that a couple of weeks ago one child had slammed into a tree at the bottom of the hill. I was not feeling comfortable about letting Chrissy go sledding on this hill! But I was tied up preparing for a meeting, so I couldn't go.

Chrissy came into my office and said, "Daddy, I want to go sledding with my friends on the hill."

I wondered how I was going to get her to understand the reasons I didn't want her to go.

"I really don't want you to go sledding there, there are two trees at the bottom, and you know me, Safety First!"

Chrissy thought for a moment, and said. "But Daddy, my friend's mom and dad are going. They're adults, so it will be safe!"

I was in a corner; there was going to be adult supervision. (Although, I've known adults who needed adult supervision!) This was going to be tough. And then a thought popped into my head!

"Chrissy, how many children do our neighbors have?"

Chrissy replied, "Five."

I then responded, "Well the deal is, they have five children. If one hits the tree and they lose one, they still have four left. Right? I only have you. Do you understand?"

Chrissy pondered for a moment "Oh, I get it. If you lose me, you won't have anyone to play with, right?"

"That's correct." And that closed the book on the issue.

I love "Child Sense", it does have some logic to it!

The neighbor family was awesome. They were always on the go and having fun. One summer evening we had them over for dinner, and we were discussing what a terrible year it had been for hornets.

I had just found a new hornet nest outside on a small tree about four foot off the ground. I was concerned about using chemicals to destroy the nest because of the dogs. My neighbor said he had a chemical free way of taking care of the nest. He said you simply go out after dark with a large garbage bag, slip it over the nest, and tie it off. No chemicals, no nest!

Well we did consume a little wine, though I'm not saying that it impaired our judgment. But it was dark, I had a large garbage bag, and off we went.

It was really dark that night! And our subdivision is completely without streetlights. When it's dark, it is a black octopus ink, shut your eyes with the lights off, fall into a well, the cave collapsed, black hole kind of dark. So I took a flashlight.

My neighbor began to slip the garbage bag over the football size nest and then it began. It started out with a little "Ouch!" then "Oh no!" At that point the language reminded me a lot of Carol's utterances during childbirth. But to his credit, he kept working the bag over the nest and then he broke off the branch and tied it up.

He only had about eight stings! It truly is impressive how men will put up with pain to prove a point!

Of course, the wives, (who were safely in the house drinking wine) saw us, and began howling with laughter! Why is it when we observe the ones we love in pain, it elicits a red-faced, gut-busting, tear-shedding, breath-gasping belly laugh?

We applied a bee sting potion, and, of course, more wine. When we moved away, I knew we would truly miss them. They were good people and they knew how to have good fun!

During this time in Chrissy's development, she had a memory like a steel trap. She memorized the movie "The Lion King" from beginning to end, with all the songs, voice inflections, everything. Then came "The Mummy," "Harry Potter and the Sorcerer's Stone,"

The Emperor's New Groove," and "Back to the Future."

What truly is impressive to me is that she could, and did, put on the entire movies, acting them out! I'm sure lots of other children accomplished the same feat, I just didn't know any. I was very proud of her accomplishments. Her memory helped her later in life with academics.

One area I have not touched on is the fact that no matter how hard parents try, no matter how much emphasis on "safety first," things still happen to children growing up.

Now, I'm not talking about deep bruising in multiple areas that make you call Social Services. I'm talking about the bumps and scrapes that just seem to happen.

I remember one time when Chrissy was young, 3 or 4 years old, and she was playing with a friend on our cement driveway. She slipped, fell, and had quite a raspberry, road-rash, or scrape on her knee. This happened while I was at work.

Well the next day, we were playing in the driveway and sure enough, while running she tripped, slipped and fell exactly on the same spot, scraping off the scab and causing a larger injury. The screaming and crying was justified and I felt the hurt, way down in my internal organs. You know, the queasy feeling you get when someone describes an operation they had?

It didn't look deep, just scraped on the surface again, so after holding her, the pain had calmed down. We took her inside, washed the wound, put a medicinal spray on it and headed out to Cook's Dairy Farm for an ice cream.

Wow, Cook's Dairy Farm, what a jewel! Located in Michigan, it is a commercial dairy farm, with the cows living on site. Cook's has a retail store where they sell their own brand of milk, butter and of course, ice cream.

Incredible edible ice cream cones! A single is more than enough for anyone. A double leaves you feeling swollen and in distress. A triple requires a professional football player-like appetite and a hippopotamus-sized mouth and stomach. I mean, it's a real pig out. The Verniers love ice cream, but a double will do!

There were not a lot of those bump and scrape incidents, a part of growing up, but I would have preferred none!

You get the same feelings when your child goes in for vaccinations. I just hate to see Chrissy in discomfort. If I could take her pain away and suffer it myself, I would!

Wouldn't any parent?

It's all a part of life.

3 ANIMALS AND MORE

The Vernier family has a deep love and respect for animals. We believe that our lives are enriched, enhanced and energized through a caring relationship with animals.

We flock to nature shows on TV. Wildlife videos are truly why HD TV was invented (along with sporting events too, for those who watch them).

Chrissy's love for animals started very early in her life. She was drawn to playing with stuffed animals. Her dolls sat in the play box-neglected much to Grandma's chagrin. Grandma built a beautiful collectable doll display and gave Chrissy several dolls hoping to generate some interest in them. While she appreciated the gifts, she just did not play with them.

Yes the world of playing with stuffed animals seemed endless. She would talk to them, sing with them and watch TV and movies with them. She would play veterinarian with them (being a veterinarian would be her initial career goal). She would sleep with them and it seemed she had an insatiable appetite for collecting more and more of them.

Carol loves animals, but specifically in those days horses, dogs and yes guinea pigs.

Chrissy's love for animals was indeed open ended, she loved them all! And believe me, she really wanted 101 Dalmatians! I, of course, did not want to pick up the scat, the poopies, the landmines, the dog logs, the puppy presents, or whatever you want to call them!

Yes, dogs do turn a backyard into a septic field if you don't keep up with their many deposits.

Humans like to personalize or humanize their animals. Disney has engrained this concept into all of us. Both cartoon characters and live movies capitalized on this movement to give all animals a human name!

Remember "Charlie the Lonesome Cougar" or "Big Ben" the bear? Or what about the really scary rat horror movie, "Ben." Think of cartoon movies like "Madagascar" or "Lion King." All are these are great movies but indeed they individualized animal characters with name's, and unique personalities.

No doubt, our animals have all had both names and their own personalities. Reviewing how we named our dogs will defy logic, question our intelligence and seem a bit silly, but here goes.

Penny seemed very expensive to us, so her registered name was "Tera Aqua Costa Pretty Penny." That seems to make some sense. Penny as you know learned the names of many toys and loved to play ball. She was a good dog.

When it came time for Penny to take her journey to doggie heaven, it was time for the Vernier's to grieve. The loss of a dog feels like the loss of a family member. We love our dogs, and it hurts when they die.

Every night I came home to crying, grieving and sadness in the Vernier household. We put money down on a golden that we could pick up in six weeks! After about two weeks of this episodic insanity, I could not take it any longer. We found a litter of golden's that were ready to go! And off we went to just "look" at the puppies! Well I'm sure you know what happened next! Carol and Chrissy wanted the puppy now!

Our new puppy was named Snowy! Chrissy was about five and wanted to name her dog. It just so happened that the day we picked her up it was snowing outside. I guess she might have been named Sunny, Rainy, Stormy, Thunder, Hail, Sleet, Cumulus, Nimbus do you really want me to go on?

Snowy became Chrissy's dog; Snowy loved her so much. I have heard of stories of the love and dedication that a dog can have for a human. One that comes to mind is the story of a little boy who was being attacked by bees and who would have been killed. The dog laid down covering the boy and took the majority of the stings. The dog died but the boy lived! When I hear of stories like this, I feel that God has truly put dogs on this earth to befriend humans. This is an example of the special bond that can be built between a dog and its human. Unbelievable! You know that "Dog" spelled backwards is God!

I understand that there are some mean dogs in the world. Yes, dogs traveling in packs have attacked humans, but I do not believe it is their basic nature to harm humans. I believe that they are on this earth to bond with and be helpmates to humans.

There are many examples of dogs working with humans. Watching a border collie herding a flock of sheep. Police dogs risk their lives, to protect their human partner from criminals.

I love the movie "Greyfriars Bobby" a Disney movie, a true story about a special bond that went beyond the boundaries of death. Every day this little Scottie dog would go to his human's grave and lay on it until nightfall. There are countless examples of the bond between a dog an its human!

This was the kind of a beautiful bond that Snowy and Chrissy developed. On a fourth of July, I lit off some legal fireworks. Snowy saw the firework go off with the noise, light and smoke and was concerned for her human. Snowy jumped on the fireworks to save Chrissy. Thankfully I was close, and I grabbed Snowy before she was harmed. I always revered that bond between them, and my respect for Snowy increased.

Well if one dog is good, two must be better! Next up is Buffalo dog! You know, that was the puppy that we put money down on but couldn't wait the full six weeks without a dog in the house!

When we brought Buffalo home, the breeder told us to keep her separated from our other golden for a week. Sure, that's an easy one!

Well we put Snowy in the family room and Buffalo in the kitchen. We placed a child gate between the kitchen and the family room. It did not take long for our new puppy Buffalo to spot Snowy!

Buffalo was determined to let nothing stand in the way of getting acquainted. She bumped into the gate, studied it for a moment, backed up several paces, lowered her head and charged! The gate went over and she ran to Snowy! Carol picked up the puppy and brought her back to the kitchen, and I replaced the gate.

The puppy repeated the charge and I said, "Gosh, she looks like a little Buffalo charging that way." And the name stuck.

Next is Princess! About five years later! My Mom always talked about getting a Bichon Frise. So I made her dream come true and bought one for her.

I called her when we were on the road and asked her and dad to meet us at our house for a surprise. A surprise they received, but not exactly what I had in mind. When we arrived at our house, we were surprised to see a police car and to hear the house alarm going off. Mom and Dad arrived at our house before us, knocked on the door and when we did not answer they opened the door and set off the alarm!

Well, they looked a little weary after their "stress test" of dealing with the noise and the police, so we ushered them into the family room. I went out and brought the little white ball of fur in to meet them!

I had told my Mom that I was getting her a Pug and Jack Russell mix: A Pussell! I have found in life that it is always fun and a positive experience to exceed the expectations of others. So she was expecting a mixed breed dog, not the Bichon Frise she always wanted!

She really did not know what to expect, she looked and said something like "She's really cute, what type of dog is she?"

I told her "She is a Bichon Frise!"

Then Mom squealed with joy and responded with all of the excitement, thrill and delight that happen when dreams come true. We then offered to keep Princess for a month to housebreak her, to make it easier on Mom and Dad, and then we would bring Princess to them and that's what we did!

A month later, we dropped Princess off at Mom and Dad's. We gave them instructions on how to keep up with the housebreaking training. (Princess did not have an accident for a couple of weeks) All was good! A week later I received a call from Dad, "Come and get this dog, she is not house trained." It was about 1:30 in the after noon.

I asked Dad when she was last let out? He responded this morning, I knew we better go and get Princess!

The first six months of training is intensive, but with positive reinforcement of course, a dog can become your best friend. That means you keep a close watch on them and if they drink, they go outside. If they eat they go outside. If they start looking around, they go outside. Essentially, they go outside a lot until the training is complete! And that is how the "Little Dog" came to live with the golden retrievers. She became my dog and we are inseparable. She is sitting at my feet as I'm writing this book. I love the companionship, the fun, and the whole dog owning experience.

All too soon our Snowy was called up to doggie heaven. It was unexpected and as always it was a sad time in our lives. We were heartbroken to lose her. Chrissy was devastated, suffering from depression, loneliness and sadness. I promised her that I would get her a new puppy, but that I had to take my time to find her a very special puppy. I knew that replacing Snowy would be a tall order! (Little did I know that a wonderful dog was just born and waiting for Chrissy!)

Our new dog was named Chloe! Her name came from the "Left Behind" books. Chloe was special from the moment we picked her up!

Chloe sat in Chrissy's lap as happy as a clam, as we brought her home. From the very first night there was no cage for Chloe; she slept in Chrissy's bed. She was house trained in a couple of days!

The two of them bonded in a way I thought I would never see again in my lifetime. They swam together, they walked together and they ran together, they went on bike rides, and roller bladed together. They played ball together, and they slept together. Chrissy even taught her to go tubing on the lake. (This always brought a lot of interest, stares, applause and laughter from other boaters on the lake!) There is a picture in the back of this book of Chloe and Chrissy tubing!

Chrissy also trained Chloe and competed in our local county fair. They loved winning Obedience and Showmanship competitions together. Chrissy and Chloe are very close. A bond this close can also cause problems. When Chrissy went off to college, Chloe had to be put on Prozac to control her "obsessive compulsive disorder!" Chloe had licked the hair completely off her paw. What a gift to have this close of a relationship twice in her life!

Our conglomeration of animals in the Vernier home did not stop with dogs. When Chrissy was in the fourth grade, she participated in a science project with a crayfish.

It was named "Cray". Well Chrissy informed us that Cray was coming to live with us when the science project came to an end. I was not sure how to keep a crayfish alive, so I went to the local pet store where they gave me some advice, sold me some turtle food and wished me luck. Cray lived in a dog bowl and seemed to be doing well for a couple of weeks.

Then one night I noticed that Cray was moving a little slowly, actually very slowly. In fact, he did not seem to be moving at all! I talked with Chrissy and suggested that Cray would be happier if we found a beautiful stream and let him go back to live in the wild.

She was ok with that and the very next day that's just what we did. We placed Cray in the stream and he seemed happy. Of course he didn't move, but he seemed happy and Chrissy was happy and that's what its all about!

A little while later it was time to have some goldfish. Chrissy named one Goldie and the other Spot! We started them out in a small goldfish bowl. Now, I don't know what type of goldfish they were, but they continued to grow and grow and grow.

We next purchased a larger goldfish tank. This was a little awkward for Carol (yes of course Carol) to clean. What to do?

It just so happened that our neighbors across the street landscaped their garden with a beautiful man-made pond! Chrissy would go over and visit Nana (The neighbors name for grandma) for hours.

What fun and what a good friend to have in the neighborhood. And what a pond! It had frogs, other pond fish and it was deep enough to be a year round pond. It would freeze over in the winter, but the fish would be deep enough, and with the help of an oxygenator to add oxygen to the water, the fish thrived.

One night, after Chrissy had gone for a visit at Nana's pond, I asked her how much she like the pond. I asked her if she thought the fish that lived there, were happy.

She loved the pond and stated that the fish were very happy living there.

So I asked her "How would you like it if Goldie and Spot would go to live in the pond? You could go over and visit them often, and they would not be lonely, like they are now when you go to school!"

She thought about it and loved the idea. I went and talked to Nana and everyone was happy. Mom was happy, Chrissy was happy, Daddy was happy, Nana was happy and of course Goldie and Spot were happy!

And now, its time to share the story "The Guinea Pig in the Freezer!" This is the story of Taffy and Malty our guinea pigs. Since Taffy was a name of a candy, Chrissy wanted a candy type name for the other guinea pig; Malty as in malt balls. The balls might have been prophetic.

Chrissy had been playing at being a veterinarian for years, first at grandma's with a stethoscope and a stuffed animal that needed fist aid and of course at home, although we did not let her bandage up our live animals.

Chrissy also played veterinarian on her computer with various games and programs. She really knew a lot about animals. Carol and Chrissy convinced me to go and buy two guinea pigs so they could both pet a pig at the same time. So off we went to the pet store! Well Chrissy picked out two very pretty pigs.

Taffy was black and brown and Malty was mostly white with brown.

"Are they male or female?" I asked.

I turned them over and could not find an M or an F anywhere. The pet store stated that they couldn't tell at this age, naturally their goal is to sell them. Chrissy felt that she could and thought that they were both females. Ok with a 50/50 chance, we bought the pigs and the cage and brought them home!

The pigs were a fun addition to the Vernier household, and seemed to enjoy the trip up north on the weekends. This went on for some time, lots of petting and "squeaking", the little noise guinea pigs make. And of course, there will be lots of cage cleaning by Carol!

The contract that cannot be broken once it is sealed with "you said" does not work when a child utters it. I guess it is because they are not at the legal age to enter into a legal contract.

Anyhow, kids will commit to anything to get a new pet into the house. But when the rubber meets the road, and the newness of the pet wears off, guess who ends up with the cleaning, feeding, vet bills etc: Mom and Dad!

As time went on, we noticed that Taffy seemed to be gaining weight faster that Malty. At first we didn't pay a lot of attention and then we noticed that she was getting really bigger. It was like living through an episode of "I didn't know I was pregnant."

But alas, Taffy was in the family way, she had a bun in the oven, she was eating for two. Yes she was knocked up, oh heck, the rabbit died! Here is that darn rabbit thing again! How to they check a rabbit to see if it is pregnant?

So we all waited for the birth of little piglets! And then one night up at the cottage, it happened. One by one the little piglets appeared. They were very small and not very furry. A total of four were born.

But then our hearts were not happy. They were still born. None of them lived. Chrissy was so sad. Carol and I felt so bad for the babies and of course Chrissy. And then it happened; we noticed that Taffy was not doing well.

We called the veterinarian, (at 5:00 in the morning), who groggily answered the phone at that hour, said that often the mother guinea pig's will often break their pelvis during childbirth and unfortunately die. This was to be Taffy's fate. She suggested giving Taffy some corn syrup. A little while later Taffy died in Chrissy's arms.

This hit her hard. It hit Carol and I hard too as the Vernier's love their pets! We try so hard to take care of our pets. In fact my best friend Eddy has always said that when he dies, he wants to come back as one of our pets!

Carol had taken the baby guinea pigs away and then went to take care of Taffy. Chrissy was not ready. After a while she took Taffy to the kitchen, took out a large freezer storage bag, placed Taffy in the bag and placed her in the freezer.

I talked to Chrissy and said we should do something else with Taffy's body and she replied in a solemn tone of voice "Dad, I don't want to talk about this now." And we didn't.

As the years progressed, I would periodically ask to take Taffy out and bury her and Chrissy gave the same response, "Dad, I don't want to talk about this now." And we wouldn't.

Over the years one thing we learned is that furry animals don't seem to get freezer burn! It also was a great conversation starter if a guest would go to the freezer for some ice for their drink. After seeing Taffy, some of them really needed their drink!

Chrissy kept saying "Dad, I don't want to talk about this now."

I hoped that a time would come and we could talk about it and Chrissy could have closure. And that time would indeed come!

Carol's love of horses was downloaded into Chrissy like a virus to a computer, with unintended (yet awesome) consequences. I remembered her first ride on a "penny" horse, at the local Meijer's store. Chrissy fell in love with the motion, the fun and the total experience. I spent a lot of time and pennies on that horse. And any other penny horse our paths would cross! I always focused a lot of time and energy on helping Chrissy to attain her goals and to grow through real life experiences.

So, naturally, when I took her to a carousel that had horses on it, her face lit up, like a like a show-ending fireworks finale! This was it! She would ride the carousel until I ran out of time, money, or both.

The next step of course is to take her all over the state to experience different carousels. Chrissy would always beeline-it to the horse on the carousel to ride on. Dozens and dozens of times, round and round she gleefully rode the noble steeds. I loved seeing her sublime happiness!

One beautiful autumn day, we took a day trip to a local children's farm that offered, of course, pony rides.

The next level of excitement and additiction took off faster than a "Duck on a June Bug" (a colloquial saying that I really don't understand.) Chrissy was mesmerized! The whole concept of a real live horse, the feel, the sight, sounds, and yes smells! She loved it all!

I did not realize that this was the beginning of a love and a lifetime of equestrian activities and expense involving the entire family. I always liked horses, enjoyed seeing them in a pasture, or on the TV westerns or movies, but my personal involvement with horses was to go light years beyond my wildest expectation.

Continuing with my theme of "safety first", even though I felt very squeamish at the thought of Chrissy on a horse, I agreed to start her in riding lessons. I found solace in the fact that she was getting excellent training.

Chrissy was thrilled! She was just under five when she had her first lesson from a stern taskmaster, an Olympian level rider! As I look back, she reminded me of the principal in the movie "Matilda!"

Chrissy was yelled at if she made a mistake during walk, trot and later canter. While the training was tough, Chrissy gave it her all. She never minded the yelling and she stuck it out. Chrissy developed a lifelong excellent seat, the ability to stay balanced in the saddle, based on this initial training.

She took lessons twice a week and her coach then moved her along into English Jumping! Yes, it scared me to think of her riding on top of a horse, jumping over anything.

Be still my heart, jumping? I was assured it was completely safe. Of course when Chrissy would take a fall, I was not told for months after the fact and the bruises were but a fond memory.

She took lessons for seven years. At first she didn't like competition, until she started winning ribbons.

I remember her first walk trot competition; she did not win a ribbon on her first three rides. She was really upset and started walking outside of the barn away from people. I walked up to her and she was in a down mood. We had a great talk about sportsmanship and how competition is a healthy learning process. We discussed how people did not like unsportsmanlike conduct and especially other people who complain when they don't win. We talked about the fact that the most important thing is to have fun, gain experience, and be known for having great sportsmanship skills. Winning ribbons or not is just a little extra fun.

She seemed o.k. And she accepted my advice. Then she went back in to compete. Well, it couldn't have worked out better if I had written the script; that day she went on to win two ribbons for her riding. Then she began cheering on other riders! Chrissy's great sportsmanship skills stayed with her the rest of her life!

At that time in our lives, we did not buy Chrissy a horse because the boarding costs in the area we lived in were very expensive. Then my company directed me to move up north for a new job. This would be very tough on Chrissy because she had many friends. So I asked her what it would take to make her happy with the move.

She thought for a little while and then answered, "I want the animal planet channel on TV and I want my own horse!"

I agreed to her requests, and so it began!

I felt very excited about the move up north and my family would learn to love it! Now as I mentioned earlier, Chrissy had taken English jumping lessons for about seven years. We came to discover that in our new northern home, English jumping was not in vogue.

We were living in the country now! It was going to be an all-new learning experience for Chrissy! Speed and action; you know, barrel racing around three barrels, pole bending, winding through poles and streaking back to the finish. Then there is keyhole where you ride up and turn your horse around without stepping out of the keyhole area. And of course flag-racing where you ride at full speed, pick up the flag out of a bucket on top of a barrel and drop it off on the other side of the course into another bucket on a barrel. Then it's time to slow down and compete in western pleasure riding, an elegant expression of horse and rider skills. This indeed was a whole new skill set for Chrissy to learn!

We set her up for lessons, with a salt-of-the-earth trainer that was into training kids because he loved it! He and I hit it off quite well. We had an immediate rapport. I knew he was doing things for the right reasons and I think he felt the same way about me.

He loved Chrissy! He loved the way that she would focus on his lessons and no matter how hard he worked her, she stayed right with it.

He mentioned that to me on a couple of occasions. He gave her a great gift of learning to love new riding disciplines.

This also was the beginning of our involvement in 4H. Chrissy joined the 4H, but to have a complete experience the family has to be involved. We did and we still do to some extent.

The 4H pledge:

I pledge my head to clearer thinking, my heart to greater loyalty, my hands to greater service and my health to better living for my club, my community, my country, and my world.

The 4H motto:

To make the best better.

I strongly recommend to all families to join 4H, it's a great fun and learning experience.

Chrissy began 4H in 7th grade. Her schedule quickly filled up. She was so busy, she didn't have time to sit down on the couch and watch her favorite TV shows. Maybe that was the best thing!

I reflected back to my schedule during 7th grade and I can sum it up quickly, I attended school.

Chrissy's schedule included 4H meetings, riding lessons twice a week, grooming her horse a couple of times a week, horse chores; and home chores. She participated in choir performances and in 8th grade she auditioned and obtained a part in a play!

Christy, Carol and I continued in 4H throughout her high school career. She competed at many county fairs and had a lot of fun. Chrissy added a lot of ribbons, medals and trophies she earned in competitions.

The real rewards are the experiences gained and the lifelong friendships with other kids, parents, and the many volunteers who enhance the 4H experience. By the way, we had a lot of fun volunteering for many 4H activities. In fact Carol and I were named 4H parent volunteers of the year in 2006. Many parents are deserving of this award; it was an honor to receive it.

We first boarded our horse. Boarding is a fun way to have a horse. When you want to ride your horse you simply go over to the stable and ride. Of course in our little town, that meant that you had to brush and tack up your horse, pick its hooves, and ride. Then you would untack the horse, brush it, pick its hooves, place it in the stall and go home and have a sandwich.

In more posh communities, they have people who do all of that for you, so you just ride. You are handed the reins and you ride and then you hand them the reins and go for lunch at the country club. Either way it takes minimum effort and its still great fun!

As we were to learn, tragedy can happen when you have horses. Chrissy's barrel horse Honey, coliced suffering a stomach ache that can cause death, broke out of her stall, entered a tack room and rolled around hurting herself in the process. This was a crisis for Honey and for Chrissy. Honey was severely hurt. Chrissy was heartbroken, and so were Carol and I.

We learned that she could be rehabilitated with a lot of time and a lot of money, but that she would never have the speed or control to be a fast barrel racer again. We were happy that she could with time be a safe walk, trot, and trail horse.

What to do? We need a barrel horse! I contacted a business associate and friend. She is gifted at connecting people with animals. She was always pairing up people with dogs, horses or whatever. She is a very experienced rider. I called her and she immediately remembered that one of her friends had a reining horse, a riding discipline that requires great skill from the horse and rider. It had been determined that the horse was not going to compete at the top level, so she would be sold. The horse had a week or two of barrel training and she showed promise.

Off we went to western Michigan to look at a new horse!

Chrissy fell in love with the new horse named Blossom. She is a beautiful buckskin dunn, a tan horse with a dark face, legs and a stripe running right down the center of her back!

Chrissy rode her and she was pretty fast. She did need a lot more training of course for barrels, but she was destined to be Chrissy's horse. Her nickname became "Awesome Blossom."

Chrissy and Awesome Blossom would win many competitions together. A lot of people thought she was a turnkey horse. A turnkey horse is one that is trained and polished to the point that the lucky kid who gets to own one goes into a competition and the horse just wins without much effort on the rider's part. A professionally trained horse is also very expensive. This was not the case with Awesome Blossom. She only had two weeks of barrel training, so Chrissy worked very hard with her and her trainer Jim. Chrissy developed her into quite a nice little barrel horse.

Sometimes in life, we give too much weight to what other people think. The truth will win out over time in most circumstances. The cream will rise to the top!

While we were in west Michigan, we also met Gus, an appendix thoroughbred. A thoroughbred and quarter horse mix.

He was for sale as a potential western pleasure horse. His color was dark brown with a white mark on his forehead. I learned later that almost every one with horses has one or more for sale or trade.

We left west Michigan with two new horses. Yep, the boarding fees tripled. The next step came from Carol and was of course the fact that we needed our own horse property, to save money. (Are you kidding?)

"What do we actually need?" I asked.

Carol said, "Some land, a little run in shed, and a fence."

That sounded reasonable at the time. So looking at three horse boarding bills, I started looking for some horse property. Where was my intuitive thinking? I should have known that "if it sounds to good to be true, it usually is!"

Ok, a little horse property, a little run in shed and a fence. So I began my search and bought the property.

And then it happened: Carol began adding in a little to the original recipe. It was something like this:

"Since we have three horses, a run in shed would simply not be enough. We really would need a stable with three stalls. More stalls would be better in case we took in boarders, so we could make enough money to pay for the horse ranch. As you know horses drink a lot of water, we really need a well.

"Now since there is no house at the horse property, we need an office that is heated for the winter and has a bathroom. A shower would be nice.

"We need to have fenced in paddocks so the horses can go out and get some air at night. We need pastures for the horses to get out during the day to run to get exercise.

"We will also need a lot of hay, and a tack room for all of the saddles, pads, bits, reins, halters, boots and stuff. Don't forget about the feed and of course the nutritional supplements, bandages, and various ointments and creams.

"We need to build a driveway, and don't forget the footings for the buildings. We must have a sawdust barn. We really need an arena for Chrissy to practice in. We also need a tractor barn, and yes we need a tractor. Our truck is not big enough for the horse trailer; we need a Super Duty at least a 250.

"Heated automatic waterers are a great idea for the winter. We need blankets for the horses and a hallway for the Ferrier to work. The Ferrier will be by about every six to eight weeks. The dentist, the veterinarian, and the chiropractor will need the hallway too.

"We will need a manure spreader. Each horse generates one ton of manure per year and we need to spread it in the field. We need a brush hog to mow the pastures twice a year. So the horses can safely eat grass in their pastures.

"And don't forget the plow attachment for the tractor to push the snow. Hey, our neighbor is selling 20 acres, this would be great for hay. Hey our other neighbor wants to sell us five more acres, we could grow crops.

"We need lights on the barn and stable. We are at the stable so much we need a refrigerator and a stove to cook on. We need some couches and chairs, maybe a futon to sleep on overnight. How about a TV for the office? We need a phone system and an alarm system for extra safety!

"Chrissy will also need new show clothes, an expensive western pleasure saddle, a barrel saddle, an English saddle, a trail saddle and a dressage saddle. We will need our own saddles too!

"Fly spray and wormer every six to eight weeks. And don't forget the yearly immunizations. Don't forget the barn cats to catch the mice that go after the feed. And of course we need cat food and a litter box!"

Well, by the time we added it up the tab, my retirement date was moved back at least five years. So much for the "Horse property, a little run in shed and a fence."

Next it came time to name the now 50-acre horse ranch. I voted for The 401K Folly! What we settle on was based on our love for dogs and horses: "The Woof & Whinny Ranch!"

4 THE MOVE 'UP NORTH'

I had been working for a new company as I was downsized from my last company.

Wow! Downsized, right-sized, restructuring, corporations come up with a myriad of terms that simply mean they can fire mass quantities of people, and not get sued. At times when a company buys another company out for its products and fires a lot of people that were valued employees, this reminds me of strip-mining, and should be regulated to protect people. Twenty years ago if someone was downsized, there was some question as to why a specific individual was down sized. Today it's just a normal business process.

People's financial lives are at the whim of corporations. It is so important that you have a contingency fund just in case. Most people do not think it can happen to them; I never did, until it happened to me! I dodged the bullet multiple times, but it can and does happen.

My boss at the time of my first annual review stated that we had agreed that I would move into my geography. We actually had no such agreement. I can back that up with my letter of employment offer. But I had learned to choose my battles in the corporate world. So then I asked that my boss do the "Acid Test" on me.

39

He asked, "What is the Acid Test?"

I replied, "Knowing what you know now about me one year later, if you had the chance to hire me tomorrow, would you hire me again?"

He was taken aback, "That's pretty direct!"

"Well, you're asking me to uproot my family and I need to know your response to the "Acid Test."

He thought for a moment and then replied, "Yes I would hire you again!"

So the adventure began.

I came home and was very excited to share the news with my family. Much to my surprise, it did not go over well at all. Carol felt we were too young to move up north. I really didn't understand.

She didn't really want to quit her job as playground supervisor at the local elementary. She really loved it! But in the end, we all agreed to move up north, and employment was of course the deciding factor.

Somebody once said "Go where the money is." So we began the planning stages for the move.

Eight years earlier, we had moved from a 4,000 square foot colonial home into a 2,800 square foot colonial. We had a basement full of extra furniture.

Now we were moving from a 2,800 square foot colonial home into a 1,200 square foot ranch home. Get the picture! We were giving extra furniture to any of our relatives that wanted it, and they still are using it as of the last time I checked.

Selling a home in any market is not usually a fun filled experience. The housing market in the Detroit area was soft, but homes were slowly selling. My logic in selecting a realtor proved to be correct.

I went to the local mortgage title company and asked them for a short list of the top real estate sales representatives that had the most closing in the last six months. They gave me three names. I scheduled appointments with all three.

One was a jovial husband and wife team. They were funny! They did not show me a plan on how they would sell my house and were not sure of the listing price because they had not had time to do the pre-work. They said they did not like to do the pre-work before getting the listing because they did not want to waste their time. But they were funny! I did not list with them.

The next was an accountant type. He showed me more data, how much comparable homes sold for, how soft the market was and wanted to price the home for $50,000 less than some similar houses sold for because of the soft market. I did not list with him.

The third was truly a charm. She was very professional, came armed with a business plan, how much she would commit to spending on marketing our home and wanted to list the home in the higher range of what similar homes sold for in the last year.

She said, "You can always come down on price, but you can't go up in price. Immediate occupancy is also an advantage for relocating executives."

I liked her style and she became our agent.

She lived up to her commitments and we sold our home in three months for a reasonable price, higher than the accountant wanted us to list for.

Let the packing begin! We gathered boxes and boxes to pack with. Our families on both sides came over to help us pack, as we had to be out in two weeks. George Carlin would have been very proud of how much "Stuff" we had to pack and bring with us. We packed and packed and packed and packed!

We had boxes that we had not unpacked from a previous move. We packed small boxes. We packed big boxes. We packed small boxes into big boxes. We packed fragile items, heavy items, folded items, books, magazines, dinnerware, silverware, glasses, mugs, cookware, TV's, phones, desks, chairs and canned pears!

We packed faxes and axes, heaters and beaters, nick knacks and bric-a-bracs, flowers and towers, fish tanks and toy banks, we even packed green eggs and ham! (Oh Dr. Seuss, I think I'm losing it.)

Yes, losing it is an integral part of moving. Moving is one of the top life stressors listed on many charts. Remember, humans really don't like change.

The reward for moving is to live in a new house, make new friends and have new fresh experiences. The difficulty is getting your "stuff" there! Many people hate moving. I just love it. The excitement of so many new experiences sights and sounds just energizes me.

One of the things that go under the heading of a "Fact of Life" is that as you get older in relation your back can't seem to handle the heavy stuff anymore. You know - like the washer, the dryer, the dressers, and the weightlifting equipment. We have a lot of exercise equipment. Unfortunately, the only thing that has downsized over the years is my bank account. Treadmills are great for hanging clothes on, as are exercise bikes. Dumbbells (named for the equipment and the purchasers of such equipment) make great doorstops.

What is another key "Fact of Life" in regard to moving? As you age is that your friend's backs are in the same stage of decay. My first move we had about 20 helpers. Second move 12, third move eight, fourth and hopefully the last move we were lucky to have six people help.

We hired a local moving company to move the majority of the heavy stuff. They did an excellent job, under challenging circumstances.

They had not seen the home that we were moving this immense collection of furniture into. That was a good thing, because they might not have taken the job!

The day of the move arrived. It was mid-February in Michigan. Up until the day of the move we were blessed with cold, but decent weather. The day of the move we were blessed with snow.

"Every day is a gift, some are just a little more fun to open than others!" This has become my favorite quote of recent years!

A fresh snowfall is a beautiful experience. The grasses, roads and trees all become coated in a glistening white beauty. You know the whole "I'm Dreaming of a White Christmas thing." If you enhance your experience with a lot of snow, say six to ten inches in a short period of time, your experience especially on moving day may be filled with the unexpected!

And so it was, the movers were packing in the snow! It snowed and snowed and snowed. Everybody's feet were cold from the snow. Our coats and gloves were wet from the snow. The driving was difficult in the snow and I was concerned about an accident due to the road conditions, but the move was on!

The movers completed loading the agreed upon items, and began their trek "up north." Of course we all know that a drive "up north" can take time, food, and lots of money!

Earlier in the day, before the movers arrived and the snow began to fly, we, along with our family and friends, had packed an enclosed trailer with the smaller items. It took three more long and tedious round trips of loading and unloading to complete the moving of the smaller items. The drive three times in one day was indeed episodic insanity!

I have to give special recognition to my family and to my best friend Eddy. Eddy spent three days and two nights helping us move. We have been friends for over 40 years. Eddy knew that I would do the same for him, if my back would hold out of course.

We then headed "up north" again, Carol and Chrissy in my van packed with stuff, and Eddy and I in the SUV packed with stuff and of course the covered trailer. I felt like one of the pioneers of the old west, heading "up north!"

We all arrived "up north" ahead of the movers, and unloaded all of our "stuff." We had eaten fast food on our journey, including some jerky, and then we waited for the movers. They arrived two hours late. I was getting very nervous, with the bad weather and all, but I felt better when they pulled up to the house.

The movers took a quick first look at the size of our home, and complained that our "stuff" wouldn't fit.

"Well, let's just begin the process and see what happens." I said.

And so the unloading began.

I felt like a triage doctor during the filming of a war scene. I was shouting out "First bedroom on the left," and "Basement" or "living room!" This went on for hours. Slowly the moving van emptied out. And slowly the movers became more irritated with where to put our "stuff". They had to stack stuff on top of other stuff and it completely filled the basement. I mean there was barely room to squeeze through to the washer and dryer or to my desk. And then they were done. All of the activity, hustle and bustle ended at last.

The moving supervisor handed me the bill and had added on $200.00 for additional handling of the furniture. I agreed with him that it was reasonable, so we wrote the check. Carol began the unpacking, and Eddy and I took the second of the three more trips back to the old house to pack up more stuff!

Eddy and I drove the two plus hours back. We talked about old times, old friends, old jokes, old songs, and we agreed that moving was getting old. That was the first 30 minutes of our trek. I assured him that this was the last time that I would ask for his help in moving. So far it has been true.

It's interesting how familiar you become with a road that you travel frequently. You get to know where the fast food restaurants are and at what exit. You learn where the least expensive jerky-laden gas stations are and, most importantly, where the rest stops are. You know you've gone this way too often when you recite stories that happened at specific mile markers.

After the additional trips, the move was over. Done, completed, that's all she wrote; the fat lady sang, conclusion, the end! Or is it just beginning?

Time to unpack. The fact is that many of the boxes we just couldn't get to. The house, specifically the basement, was so stuffed with our stuff; we just could not get to all of it. So, we took our time, worked on unpacking over the next few years, well decades, well actually we still have not unpacked it all. It is a work in progress!

To all of my friends and family that have helped us move through the years, thank you!

And in the future, if you need help with your moving, I will be glad to help. I will give you the phone numbers of several movers, I will help you interview the movers, and I will make the pizza and beer run on moving day!

A move and unpacking is truly just the beginning. There is so much to learn about your new environment. First up is finding all of the local eateries, food as mentioned is a bit of a focal point for the Vernier family. Next you need to find out where to shop and where to go to school for Chrissy. Then you have to locate your chosen church and of course the local watering holes.

I felt like Chevy Chase in the movie "Funny Farm." All new places to go and people to meet! At times being new to an area can make you feel a little out of place. The people of the community quickly made us feel at home.

Yep, we were city mice and now we are country mice. There are a lot of differences between the city and the country. Driving in the city is measured by time, not miles. The distances from point A to point B are not usually a lot of miles.

Driving in the country is measured by miles, not time. The distances from point A to point B are usually a lot of miles!

The city has clearly marked streets, large malls, posh areas to live in if you can afford it, and of course areas of the city to avoid (crime, drugs, hookers). The city has cultural experiences such as opera, symphony, Broadway plays, and gourmet dining. There is a lot of traffic to avoid, zillions of people, leash laws, pooper-scoopers, noise ordinances and unusual odors. There are conveniences like city sewers and water. There is talk radio, rap stations, jazz stations and pop music stations. People are stressed out and always in a hurry. With all of its sophistication, I sometimes felt that city life was unnatural.

The country has unmarked streets, no malls, some posh homes, areas of the country to avoid, fresh manure fields, parades, Amish road apples, and dollar stores. The country has cultural experiences; demolition derby's, tractor pulls, county fairs, cow tipping (should that be 15 or 20%?). There is Country dining and farm machinery and Amish neighbors to avoid on the roadways. You will find less people, no leash laws pooper-scooper or noise ordinances. There are of course weekenders with stereo's and fireworks. "Up North", the Fourth of July goes from May to September.

We have unusual odors, septic systems, and wells. I remember my sister in-law asking how the septic system and well actually work.

I told her that when you flush the toilet, it goes into a hole in the ground in the backyard. Then it travels to the front yard and you pump it up into the house from another hole in the ground. That did it for her; she never drank the water from our house again.

There is Religious radio and country music. People are relaxed and never in a hurry. The area in Michigan where we live has an Amish population. I felt very comfortable with that. I've watched the movie "Witness" with Harrison Ford and the movie "For Richer or Poorer" with Tim Allen. Yep, I know that we are the "English" and I am familiar with terms like shunned, ordinands, plain and "bake sale."

We have Amish neighbors. In our area, the Amish do not use electricity. This fact shocked Chrissy. Imagine, no TV, electronic games, CD's, DVD's blue-ray, phones, and no I-phones or Blackberry's. To us it's like living in the Stone Age! To the Amish, it's a more peaceful and God like lifestyle.

Meeting new people in the winter "up north" can be a bit challenging. At our home on the lake, in the winter is not exactly a hub of activity. At this time of year, there are only about 30% year round residents "up north."

The rest are city mice making a living at their year round residences. Many people in the winter months shut down their cottages. They have the water pipes blown out, and turn off the heat. They come back in the spring to turn on the water, find the new leaks and get ready for summer.

We also have what are known as the "Snow birds". These fortunate people have an additional home in Florida or "down south." Just like many of their ornithological friend's, they participate in the great migration south for the winter and they will return in the spring!

So, here we are, we just made a permanent move. We live 14 miles from town and it's winter. Yes it is a cold desolate and lonely existence. The only people we knew "up north" have shut down their cottages. My family felt isolated and began having second thoughts about the decision to move "up north."

We decided to go out to dinner and dined at a restaurant that we had enjoyed on the weekends called Hunter's. We each had a very good meal. The waitress was friendly, the service efficient. I paid the bill and we were in the process of leaving the restaurant, actually, we were just heading out of the second door and as the cold air hit us, I was reminded that I did not have my hat!

Now considering that I am a bit san's pate, living with the fringe, a partial skinhead, a baldy, sporting a solar panel, chrome dome. As they say "God only made a few perfect heads, and the rest he covered up with hair!" I felt it quick when it was cold out. I also knew first when it was just starting to rain. I quickly turned around and instantly was halted when I ran smack dab into a really big man! He was tall, almost seven foot tall. He was big, really big - a John Candy from the movie "The Great Outdoors" Big, Big, Big, Tall, hard, I can hear the Jimmy Dean song "Big John" playing in my mind. You know, it kind of took my breath away!

Not knowing what to expect next, I said; "Excuse me, I'm sorry!" And then waited for the punch, a beating or some response.

"Big John" looked down at me and in a soft voice, he then said, "It's ok, you're forgiven."

I felt relieved; I backed out of his way and watched him walk out toward his pickup truck.

Carol said " Geeze Joey, be more careful."

I went back in and retrieved my hat. Little did I know that in the future the "big man" was actually a gentle giant; his family, and mine would become friends. He and his wife are truly among the most charitable people I had ever met!

Moving to a small town "up north" in mid-Michigan was certainly a change in life style. We moved from an area that was two miles from high school, church, and groceries.

The Great Lakes Shopping mall was five miles away. Pine Knob in winter offered downhill skiing and in summer offered a fantastic concert series. We had our famous franchise restaurants and several independent restaurants ranging from the coffee shops to some gourmet dining experiences.

Now we were literally fourteen miles or more to town. We do have a McDonalds and a Burger King, but the Taco Bell closed down Too bad we love Taco Bell. We are a small town. No K Mart, but a Pamida opened up, that is now a Shopko. We are blessed with lots of churches of different faiths.

Going to town takes planning and a real commitment.

We joined the local church that we had attended part time on our commutes. I felt very comfortable and at home. One thing I noticed is that this church loves to sing. I appreciate the energy from the congregation. It is indeed a personal preference for me to have music during services. I love the church, the people and grew to love each of the pastors, or at least most of them.

At the early mass one day, I was walking out and was surprised when I spotted, you guessed it "Big John." I went up to him to apologize again, and he asked if we were living in Gladwin or if we were weekenders. I told him we were residents now.

He said, "Well if you still feel bad about bumping into me, you could make it up by joining the "Knights of Columbus.""

The "K of C" as it is known, has its origins with Father McGivney, as a way to help widows and families who needed support. It has evolved into one of the largest fraternal organizations and insurance company's in the United States Insurance is for members only. In addition it is a charitable organization, giving support to many projects of all faiths, as well as local schools, city, scouting, and many other good causes.

I thought it would be a great way to get to know people in the community, so I joined! And I have served at many fish dinners, ever since! I enjoy the activity, and working with the different causes that will benefit from every plate sold!

I would be remiss without commenting on two of the several pastors that we were blessed with at our parish.

One pastor was a nice young man. (It seems as I get older there are a lot younger people. In fact, most of the doctors, remind me of "Doogie Howser MD.") He was very competent and I loved his sermons. He did however, have a couple of idiosyncrasies. On our annual dinner and benefit night he would dress up as a leprechaun because the theme was the "Pot of Gold". Everyone enjoyed his good spirits.

Also every Halloween, he would decorate his house in a terror movie "Jason" theme. He would then don the hockey mask, and in the best "method acting" style, he would totally throw himself into the role. Under no circumstances would he break character. The teens loved it; the younger children were a little scared. It struck me as a little on the edge! I'm sure it was a great catharsis, after being a positive role model all year long!

There are times in your life and people you meet that you sense that you are in the presence of greatness, holiness and happiness! When Father Jeff entered the room, you knew you were embraced by all of that and more. He was like a magnet drawing people of faith back to church. He was an accomplished musician, and his sermons were effortless, filled with an incredible depth of messages and enjoyable. He had a sense of humor that blended a positive message with the right touch of laughter. He visited people's homes, broke bread, and showed how much he really loved people. And we loved him!

One Saturday evening, during mass celebration, the unthinkable happened; Father Jeff had a heart attack. I received a call from one of my dear friends, who had helped with CPR until the ambulance arrived.

He was stabilized at our local hospital, and then taken to Saginaw, a bigger city, to be cared for. We were all stunned. It did not seem possible. I remember that evening, praying for Father Jeff, asking God to help him through this challenge, and to return him to us in good health. In an intuitive moment, in my mind, I envisioned Father Jeff, smiling as always and looking very happy. I imagined him, in that moment, speaking to me saying, "Joel, thank you for your prayers, but don't worry, I'm very happy, this is what I prepared for all my life! This is my moment! I'm at peace! I'm going to be where I belong! Joel, this is truly sweet!" I understood, I was sadden and happy at the same time. The next day I learned that he had passed. Heaven is enriched with his humor, many talents, and his love!

∽

Our move "up north" meant that Chrissy would enter the seventh grade midyear. I know that this was tough on her, having to leave her friends. As we promised she did get the Animal Planet channel and we were looking into the horse situation. Her new school system was much smaller than the one we left. One of my concerns was that we moved from a large suburban school to a small country school and I wanted to know the percent of kids that would go on to college. I did talk with the principal and asked her that question, and she stated that the numbers would be smaller but that the percentage would be the same.

One of my core beliefs is that all kids with the desire and competency should have the opportunity to attend college. The government talks about investing in our future, this is the single most important investment we can make. Funding should not be a roadblock.

I compliment the Kalamazoo, Michigan area that has made that happen! Children growing up in that area will have their first four years payed for with this program.

This should be available to all children, the payback to society in general is immeasurable, and would help us compete in the global market!

Chrissy made a lot of new friends. There is an advantage to being the new kid in school; everyone wants to know all about you. She fit in well, and soon the sleepovers were in full swing!

Sleepovers for kids are great, but for parents they really make you lose sleep. When kids are younger you can control the time they go to bed, but you can't control what time they stop laughing and giggling. This seems to go on forever! What is it that 7th graders can find so fascinating to talk about till two in the morning (High Schooler's until 4 in the morning). It might have been boys, horses, clothes, teachers, other kids, sports, cheerleading etc. At this age they seem to giggle in unison, they also seem to cry in unison if something strikes them as sad, wrong, or an injustice like a boy not liking one of them.

All I was interested in was getting some sleep! This became accentuated when it became summer; I had to work in the morning! "GO TO SLEEP!" I would yell out in exasperation! A little while later, the giggles would resume.

When we added on an addition to the house, I asked the architect to design a bedroom over the garage where Chrissy could have her sleepovers and I could have peace and quiet.

Eddy, my best friend, installed an alarm system so that I could be alerted if the door to the extra bedroom was opened. Ronald Reagan said, "Trust but verify" and I did just that. It was paradise; I could sleep at night again!

Living on the lake, Chrissy had a lot of sleepovers! I was happy that she was making friends so easily.

The summer went by uneventfully, Chrissy continued having friends over. We had many guests, our family and friends, and visits with our dear pals Shelley and Larry who were weekenders on the other side of the lake. It was a great summer!

The next thing we knew, it was September and time to go back to school. Chrissy, Carol and one of her friends went shopping for school clothes. The best way to describe parents and grandparents when it comes to what style is at that age is "clueless."

We have no idea what pre-teens and teens think is stylish. Keep in mind that there needs to be some limits on style. Many schools have a dress code, and of course parental consent on attire is defiantly appropriate, but please base it on today styles not from your days styles.

Keep in mind that when it comes to birthdays, Easter, Christmas or anytime, a gift card is most appropriate if you want to give clothing. I really do not like to give gift cards, but this is my exception.

I remember school shopping when I was young; it consisted of two pairs of pants, three shirts, tennis shoes, fall, spring, summer and winter shoes, of course just one pair for all seasons, and a winter coat. Yes I would jokingly tell Chrissy; "When I was young, I walked five miles to school. The walk was uphill, both ways!" or "We used to eat bean sandwiches. And we were glad to have them!" and "I used to take the top off the ice cream tub so I could play "Frisbee" with it! We didn't have a color TV, CD, DVD or electronic games!" Yep "A widescreen was on the picture window, to keep out the flies and mosquitoes!" "A hard drive was taking a trip in the summer in a car without air conditioning!" "A digital calculator was using your fingers on both hands!"

Chrissy would joyfully ask, "Were you Amish Daddy?"

Ok, maybe I stretched the stories a little.

Let's agree though, kids today have way too much stuff and their parents have way too much debt!

The average U.S, household credit card debt was $15,762 in 2015! Wow!

As a sales manager, I have the privilege to check expense reports on a monthly basis for the direct reports. On one occasion, the employee accidently sent me his credit card bill. He was the sole breadwinner in the household, with an income of $45,000 a year. The credit card balance was $38,000 dollars.

I thought to myself, good luck paying that off! Getting in debt is so easy to do! Mailboxes are stuffed with credit card offers. Some offers even come to pets that live at a home! Banks give you cash incentives to open a credit card account. Some cards give you (your) money back every time you use their cards. Of course the interest rates have soared. If you put your money in the bank in a regular savings passbook, you might earn up to 1%. Credit card companies can charge over 24% if you are late on a payment it can go even higher. Wow! No wonder it's so hard to pay off this type of debt.

If you find yourself in this situation, a great place to start is Dave Ramsey's "Financial Peace University". There are lots of other resources to help you out.

Don't let financial issues destroy your life. Get help, it will all work out if you take positive action! Most domestic arguments are about money!

8th grade was another opportunity to get to know more kids. Chrissy participated in choir and loved it. She has always loved to perform. She is self-confident on stage, and this began at an early age.

I was going to San Francisco for a meeting, and we thought we would add to it and make it a vacation. So off I went to the meeting and on the Friday the meeting ended, Carol and Chrissy flew from Detroit to San Francisco. Chrissy was about five at the time.

What a town! The trolley cars are so much fun to ride, and the new sights, new sounds and new tastes, it is a city that begs you to experience it in person and makes you want to come back for more. We stayed right downtown in a hotel.

I quickly learned that going out after dark with a five year old, was not the best idea. The people seemed to become more colorful after dark. Some wore tights, and they were, well tight, anatomically speaking. So we decided to enjoy the city in daylight hours. There should have been a sign up that states "No lewd behavior until after 12:00 a.m." I guess that's why Disney Land was created. Too bad, it is such a great city.

We took a day trip to Muir Woods. There are giant redwoods, they are so tall they seem to reach to the sky! The soft forest floor was so neat to walk on, every step you took the spongy floor would push your foot up like a mini trampoline.

As I looked up toward the treetops, it reminded me of the same feeling that hit me when as a teenager my family visited the Grand Canyon in Arizona, I felt like I was in a grand church! The beauty, the panoramic views, it was an awesome experience!

We took a tour of Alcatraz Island. Its great to put on movies like "Escape from Alcatraz" and "The Rock". During many scenes you can yell out "I was there!" I'm glad we were there just for a tour because it was an eerie place! The dampness, stillness in the air and yet you could sense the toll it took on its prisoners. Imagine the mind numbing pacing, loss of freedom and the slow passage of time eating away at your existence. Time that you lose and will never have back. Time away from family and friends, time just draining away your life. A nice place to visit, but I wouldn't want to live there!

Next we were off to visit the famous "Fisherman's Warf". I love seafood, there were many vendors and the food was great!

We noticed that a show was going to start on the wharf in about 30 minutes. We walked and observed (and smelled) the sea lions that had taken over areas of a marina. They were awesome to watch. They played, slept, fought and were a great tourist attraction!

Then we went to watch the show. Two comedic jugglers, put on a very entertaining show. There were about one hundred people in the audience. At one point in the act, the jugglers solicited a volunteer in the audience to come up on stage and participate.

At first no one noticed a little raised hand of a child that wanted to volunteer. Then all of a sudden, I noticed the little hand going up next to me, it was Chrissy!

The jugglers gratefully invited her up on the stage! She looked very comfortable. They asked her various questions, she confidently responded and they continued on with the act. Essentially they were doing some juggling tricks throwing their props, such as bowling pins, around under and over her, talking and making jokes. They noticed my concern, I kept my eye on the bowling pins, large tools and such that if they hit Chrissy, I would have jumped on stage and juggled the objects directly at the jugglers at a high rate of speed, (safety first).

They commented that I had nothing to worry about, that they were professionals, but they did state that they did not want to get beat up if they slipped and hit her with a prop! The audience loved it! And they applauded for Chrissy when she left the stage!

Positive reinforcement is a powerful force. From then on Chrissy would volunteer at every opportunity. This made our trips to Disneyland and Universal theme parks very entertaining. It also opened up a lot of opportunities going forward in Chrissy's life!

As 8th grade progressed, I detected that Chrissy was gaining friends, but wanted to get to know more kids at a faster rate.

The addition consisting of the laundry room and the garage was finally completed. It was February and a thought popped into my head, a party for Chrissy and her new friends. Of course not just any party, a "Beach Party!" The planning began, the garage was finished, insulated and had a commercial heater, so that was selected as the site.

I went on line and ordered out several "Beach oriented movies" such as; "Beach Blanket Bingo" and "How to Stuff a Wild Bikini," you know the genre. I used a video projector and showed them on a white wall.

We also ordered out lots of table decorations, fish, shells, lays, and palm trees. We had games like air hockey, basketball shoot, beanbag toss etc. We had karaoke and of course dancing. We had snacks and of course, pizza!

It was a hit, and Chrissy made many new friends! It was lot of work and a lot of fun! It is one of those little memories that makes you smile as you reflect back on your life. I was so happy that the party was such a hit. Many of Chrissy's attendees became her friends, and they are still friends to this day.

5 LAKE LIFE

I have always loved lakes. Being on the water, swimming, boating, rafting, floating or just looking at water has been a passion for me all of my life! There must be a primordial kinship to water; after all we are made mostly of the water in our cells!

I grew up in a sports crazed house. My dad would have loved ESPN and all the sporting channels that we have today. I'm glad that they were not available when I was growing up, I'm sure dad would have parked in front of the TV and would have loved to have spent the two decades of his retirement right on the couch! When there was a sport on TV, (in those days channel's 2,4,7,9 and 50), we had to stay home and watch it. We could not go anywhere, or watch anything else. When a sporting event was on TV our lives came to a screeching halt, in front of the TV. As a child and a teenager, it was very frustrating. Dad worked hard all of his life, seven days a week. I understand better now, but back then it frosted me.

In the summer I always wanted to go to the public swimming area at the "Old Homestead". It was wonderful. It cost $5.00 per carload, which back then was a lot of money, but you could stay until dark. On Sundays sometimes in the summer, when there was no sporting event on TV, we would go. We had an old army surplus tent that dad would put up for us to change, play and take naps in. The beach was sandy, the water was clear and you could see fish in near the beach!

I loved to fish. So my Dad found me a stick, tied on some string and told me to go fishing. I was about age 4. My brother Doug spotted a dead fish, he swam over and got it, while I was being distracted by my other brother Larry, and he tied the dead fish to the string! (There was of course no hook on the string). But I thought I caught a fish! I was so proud! I felt that I was a lucky fisherman and that feeling stayed with me for years, in fact decades until they told me how I caught a fish without a hook!

I have so many fond memories. Once Larry climbed up a big ugly gnarly tree, he felt like he was king of the mountain! When he began to climb down, he found that the tree had some kind of pickers on the branches; he didn't notice them when he climbed up the tree, but he found them in a hurry when was headed back down. He would move down and yell ouch! And of course since we loved him so much, we would laugh to tears! This descent went on for 10 minutes; I nearly peed in my swimsuit I laughed so hard. He made it down eventually.

I just loved summers and our visit to "The Homestead". When we did get to go, it was a day of adventure, swimming, picnicking and fun that lasted until dark.

Doug is an artist at woodworking, he has always loved it. He must have gotten this from Grandpa Ray on my dad's side. He could build anything and so could Doug. When I was younger, Doug built a boat in his basement. This was a small hydroplane; it was cool to see it develop from its frame up into a completed boat, quite an accomplishment! However, when building a boat in the basement, one does not always think about moving the boat out of the basement! One might not measure the door to see if it will fit! I came over to help him move the boat out of the basement, and we tried several different angles to fit the boat out but to no avail. For many people, this would be a crisis, but not for Doug. He measured and cut the doorframe opening to accommodate the dimensions of the boat, and it was moved out of the house!

He took me on a camping trip to Oscoda, Michigan to swim and to go for a boat ride. The boat was a beauty! When Doug took off and went top speed I felt like I was traveling at light speed. The water looked different and seemed to stand still as we shot across the lake. I loved the entire experience. I learned what S'Mores were, and decided that camping and boating were a perfect pastime!

My love of the water was enhanced when Larry rented a home on Pontiac Lake in Michigan. Larry, his wife and three children lived there right on the lake. They would have us over often, and I was infatuated with the fact you could just walk out the front door, and jump off the dock into the water! This was truly nirvana! When they moved out, my parents rented the house for the summer and I was sold. One of my goals in life was to live on the water! Looking at the water, with the sun shimmering off it, floating on a black inner tube, rowing in a boat, swimming and fishing. I loved it all and I still do.

❧

The least expensive way to be on the water was to go camping. I loved camping. I started out camping with my high school friends. Our first experience at camping started off with a very unusual problem. We set up the tent that we had bought at Sears. It took about 30 minutes to get the poles just right. Then, when we went to put the sleeping bags in the tent we found a problem. Believe it or not, there was a tent all set up with no door to enter into the tent! We walked around all four sides and then we realized the problem. We lost a half the day driving back to Sears. At first they did not believe us so we had to set it up and show them. They exchanged the tent and off we went to have a fun weekend.

Carol, my wife, and I loved to camp. At first we were lucky, we picked campgrounds that attracted real campers. You know, REAL CAMPERS! They cooked at the campsite, hung around the campsite, they built fires at the campsite and at dark, they sat around the fire telling stories and enjoying fellowship.

Not all camping experiences were so idyllic. I remember camping on Lake Michigan with Larry and his family. (If you haven't visited the Great Lakes, put it on your "bucket list!") It was a "chamber of commerce" Michigan weekend, blue sky, warm days and cool nights!

It was going great, sandy beach, beautiful night, and then around 11:00 p.m., a van pulled out, set up a tent, brought out guitars and amplifiers and proceeded to rock the campground! This went on till 3:00 a.m. My head was pounding, my heart was pounding, and I was hoping that the instigators would get a pounding, just to stop the noise. I think the mixture of alcohol and drugs put them to sleep, and the next morning I noticed that their heads were pounding, justice at last.

The next experience was at a campground in northern Michigan. Carol and I set up camp on a hot August night and went to sleep. An hour later a big camper pulled up, plugged in and cranked on their air conditioner. The noise kept us awake all night!

It's interesting that some people seem to go to get away from it all, except they seem to bring it all with them. Color TV, dishwasher, air conditioner and the whole queen bed thing.

We could have camped at the primitive sites, but Carol refused to go anywhere without flush toilets. The walk to the water closets was too far at night.

Being DINKS, (Double Income No Kids), we were very focused on Penny our golden that I discussed earlier. You've seen young people that engage in episodic insanity, they get a little species specific confused, and the dog becomes essentially their child! They are so busy with their careers or just cannot have kids so pooch is it! That was Carol and me with Penny. We were both very involved with our careers. Penny was very spoiled which is usually the case. Penny loved to swim! Michigan

54

with all of its water has very few public places that you can take your dog swimming. There are so many lakes and with the Great Lakes so much shoreline, almost all with signs, "No Dogs on Beach!" Most dogs love to swim, but unless you are a waterfront property owner, it's really hard to find water for them to play in!

If you own your own lake property your doggie can swim any time! Well for many people that's simply not an option, a second home is expensive, and most folks are having a tough time holding onto their first home today! To the State of Michigan, listen up! More dog friendly parks on the water would be great for the communities and for the tourist trade. It would be a kind of a canine stimulus package. While there are some Dog Beach parks, based on the number of dogs living in Michigan homes, the more the better.

So, we were on the hunt for a cottage!

In Michigan, in good economic times, waterfront property was pretty pricy. Carol and I would schedule weekly a little trip to learn about different lake areas in the state. At times it was disheartening. The costs were prohibitive. Then one of the people that I worked with invited us, including Penny our Golden, to come up to a small lake in mid-Michigan for the weekend to check it out!

Shelley and Larry are very dear friends. It was Larry and Shelly, who first introduced us to their lake in the fall of 1989. We woke up in the morning to a beautiful blue sky, and a sunny but crisp fall day. Larry took us out in the boat, to view the colors that were at peak on the trees.

Carol and I were hooked, and so was Penny, she swam for hours and played with Shelley's golden "Nugget". The two golden's really played well together! The only thing more pungent that one wet dog, is two or more wet dogs!

We ended up buying a small cottage the very next July. Shelly and Larry also gave us the gift of having essentially an extended family. I'm blessed again and our lives are enriched, by knowing people that are so grounded in faith and charity. They welcomed us into their family gatherings.

"Aunt" Shelly is a weekender, but her weekends are jam packed with fellowship, constant activity, and hospitality. All are welcome to come to the cabin. Every visit included family members, friends, and often members of their Marriage Encounter group!

No matter the size of the crowd, there was always plenty to eat and fun to be had.

Chrissy loves this close-knit extended family. She was especially excited when "Aunt Shelly" would come up, and stay for the summer, as many other children would soon arrive to play with. And play they did.

55

Life on a lake for a child is fun filled, swimming, fishing, boating, tubing, skiing, jet skiing, deer shinning at night with flashlight's and of course Shelley's specialty "Snipe hunting".

"Snipe hunting" was instituted whenever a new youngster of a worthy age came for a visit. Once initiated you could hardly wait for the next victim, person to be initiated into the game. Late at night, you would go out with pillowcases, to catch and keep the "Snipes" in. You simply pick a spot in the road, pull over, and everyone gets out to hunt. At night in the dark there are lots of hidden noises, Shelly would say 'Quiet, let's listen.' Then they would get out some noise-makers and callers to flush out the Snipe, a small furry animal.

Then someone would yell out 'Look out a "Snipe" is heading your way!' and everyone would scream and begin running because it was a "Big" one! This would go on for 20 minutes, and then the hoax would be let out of the bag, along with any "Snipes". One very late night, a Snipe got lose in the car and chaos ensued. What fun!

Deer Shining is an event that "Weekenders" just love to do. You go out late at night on a road with open fields. You take with you a high-powered flashlight and shine it into the fields. Deer look up at the light and their eyes shine back reflecting the light. Then, you count and keep up the tally for the night. On some nights it might be 20 to 30 deer. On a good night 60 to 100+ deer. A slow night you may see only one or two, very disappointing. It truly is great entertainment.

It is important to remember that many of the fields have nearby homes. You must never shine the light into the homes, it is important to always be respectful of other people's property.

❧

The campfire is a tradition on the lake. Although with the advent of the mosquito born West Nile Virus and the Zika virus, I shunned having too many (Safety first!"). The campfires can range from a small fire pit to the bonfire style! Some fires are so big, you can feel the heat when you pontoon by them!

One of our relatives who prided himself on being a campfire master (arsonist more likely) strived to be able to light his fires with a single match.

He built a large woodpile and sure enough it lit with one match. Of course the fire was so intense and large that it singed the branches of the pine trees 12 feet above the fire!

One New Years Eve, we were invited to attend a campfire on the lake. Yes ON THE LAKE! The campfire was built out on the ice. Now does that seem reasonable to you? We all sat around a roaring fire, off shore about 25 yards. The fire was very hot, and really kept us warm! The fire did not melt through the ice (heat travels up I guess?) but it did melt the top of the ice and your boots eventually were covered with about 3 inches of water. About then I felt it was time to go (Safety first!)

There are many stories about the weekenders that decided to light their fires with gasoline! You can see them in town shopping or at the eateries. They have a stunned glaze on their faces; they are sans eyebrows, any hair on their hands or arms and have a dark complexion. They also smell a bit smoky! It's a hard lesson, usually corrected after the first experience!

My daughter bought a jet ski with her own money when she was nineteen. Chrissy saved money from a part-time job she worked in town. She loves riding it and so do I. But many people that ride them have no clue that they are to be piloted under the same rules as a boat.

Many "Week enders" who would never think of driving a boat, jump on a jet ski and go full bore across the lake! For some reason, they lend their jet ski to young kids who have no clue as to the regulations and have never taken a boater safety course. They need to watch their distances between boats and not come too close to the back of the boat to jump the wake. Please don't go too fast near the shore where people are swimming. And especially do not jet in front of a moving boat, spin around and fall off, right in front of an oncoming boat. Also, please do not run so close to the boat that you spray people with your wake!

There is a lot of data on "Road Rage" but Jet Ski ineptness has generated a lot of "Nautical Rage!" We would even joke about a new sport "Jet Skeet Shooting!" Using paint balls to get Jet skiers attention! Be careful; remember you are essentially driving a car with no brakes! Have fun, be safe and come home alive!

Living on the lake, you are obligated to have "Lake Toys!" The list includes: life jackets for all sizes to make sure all of the guests are covered. Water lounges, floating toys, water guns and swim belts. Also multiple swim suits, towels, sun tan lotion, hats, sun glasses, more towels, sandals, bug spray, extra clothes, first aid kit, and of course food and beverages for guests!

A pontoon boat is a must, to go out for leisurely rides around the lake. A speedboat for tubing, skiing, knee boarding and to run up to the marina for a pizza. Of course a paddle boat, a fishing boat or canoe, fishing poles and equipment, and don't forget the jet ski. And remember if it has a motor, it needs to be licensed and insured! And don't forget the cleaning, covering, and putting the boats away for winter storage. All of this is very costly.

Under the heading of "Safety first!" When we were weekenders, we enrolled Chrissy in swimming lessons. She was young, under two years old. My intuitive brain, felt that if there would be a time that Chrissy fell off the dock and Carol or I would not be around. In fact this event did occur, although I was not told about it for years. Chrissy was standing on the dock looking into the water and she fell in! She recanted the story to me that she remembered not to panic, and to begin swimming to shore.

She learned that technique at her swimming lessons. She was very glad she had taken those lessons. I recommend swimming lessons for everyone who is either new to swimming, or would like to improve their swimming skills, or learn water survival techniques.

∾

The Lake offers year round fun and a variety of activities. The color tours in the fall are breathtaking. Winter is full of new activities; ice-skating on the lake can be fun, especially if you get really cold weather, then a hard freezing rain that glazes the lake smoother than a "Crispy Crème" donut! You can skate for hours and miles with a glassy path in front of you. Hans Christian Anderson would be in his element!

Most of the time, the ice freezes and then it snows. The snow blower is the ticket. You simply go out and design your ice skating rink with your snow blower!

It can be a little tricky getting the heavy snow blower down to the ice, but with some effort, you can create a nice skating rink. Then it's time to have fun!

If you have a steep drop from the bank to the water, it makes for great sledding! You slide down the bank and out on the lake. If you have blown the snow off you can travel a long way on your sled.

And of course, "Ice Fishing!" I never understood ice fishing; after all you can make your own ice, or buy it in bags from the gas station. Just kidding! What fun! Take a cold, snowy wind blown day, drag all of your equipment onto the ice, drill a hole to fish through, attach your bait to your tip up pole and wait for dinner to swim up and get hooked!

Another case for episodic insanity is the practice many ice fishermen have is to drive their truck or car on to the ice, drill a hole and fish! Just think of all the weight of a vehicle sitting on the ice! Added to this practice is the fact that the minute your vehicle rolls on the ice, your insurance is null and void. If your vehicle goes through the ice, you are essentially up the creek with out a paddle! (I'm not sure how that applies, after all if you're up the creek, wouldn't the current take you back down the creek?) You also have to pay to have your vehicle salvaged, along with various fines and fees.

I do not have all of the equipment such as a deluxe shanty, like the ice fisherman have in the movie "Grumpy Old Men". I guess if I indeed were all decked out like the movie it would be more enjoyable, and particularly if Ann Margaret was part of the package!

At Houghton Lake in the winter they have a festival called "Tip Up Town" Imagine a carnival like atmosphere that features fun, food, snowmobiles, lots of shanties, ice fishing and truckloads of adult beverages!

In Michigan, my understanding is, that you can't set up your tip up and go in the house to keep warm, you must be outside with your tip up. I only ice fish for a limited amount of time, until I get cold. Boy that 30 minutes seems like an eternity on the ice!

I have developed a lot of empathy for the practice of the Eskimo women in

58

ancient times when they became a drain on the village resources, they would go out and sit on an ice flow and drift off to oblivion! (Must be some kind of government health care program!)

I also only have a hand auger. After I get done drilling through the ice I'm ready to go home! After a bone chilling 30 minutes on the ice, there is nothing like the feel of a steaming hot shower then sitting on the couch in front of the fireplace, with under a warm blanket and sipping on a hot cocoa!

For those that love to ice fish, have at it! I salute you from my warm spot on my easy chair, and oh, by the way, please invite me over for the fish fry!

∾

The words "Sand Bar" around the Vernier house elicit a variety of noises and emotions. It's a little like yelling "Fire" in a theatre, it should almost be illegal to say the words "Sand Bar!", "Treat!" or "Let's go for a walk!" out-loud!

The dogs are the first to react. They jump up in a blinding furry flurry of agitation. Your ears are overloaded with the sounds of dogs yelping, barking, whining, whimpering, shaking, and literally coming unglued! It reminds me of the golden in the "Bacon" commercial! You can hear them thinking, IT'S "SAND BAR" TIME!

Buffalo is the all time champ when it comes to getting excited about going to the sandbar, she just loves going there to fish. She will walk up and down the sand bar looking for fish, hunting fish, planning to get fish, even though she has never caught a live fish in her life! I did take a lesson from Doug and placed a dead fish by her so she could find it and catch it. She was so proud!

Chloe our youngest golden loves going to the "Sand Bar" to play fetch. We take a "Chuck it" and throw the ball as far as we can, Chloe bounds through the water, retrieves the ball and bounds back to us to repeat the fun. Chloe is a little obsessed with fetching, catching, carrying, finding, chewing on, squeaking, and doing anything with a ball!

She also goes nuts over a red laser light! You place the red dot on the floor just a few feet away from her and the fun begins! The game is to keep the red dot just ahead of her so that she keeps chasing it! At the end of the romp, you let her catch it by turning it off when she lunges for it, and praising her "Good dog Chloe! You got it!"! What fun!

Princess, our little Bichon, also loves to go to our favorite spot on the water. Her legs are a little too short to let her just walk around as she would have to swim the whole time, so we put her on a blue water float and I tether it to my leg. She really loves to run back and forth on the blue floaty and yip loudly! She will jump off the float, realizing that she can't touch bottom and head back to the float. This goes on until she is just shaking from the cold water!

We then dry her off, and cover her with a towel. A little while later, she is ready to get back on the blue float and do it all over again! Princess grew up with two big doggies, so she believes with all of her heart, she is a big golden retriever.

For me the "Sand Bar" has always been a fun destination. It provides a safe water environment for the dogs, Chrissy and many of her friends to play on. We have enjoyed years of throwing a Frisbee, a ball, hunting for pretty rocks and shells, and simply relaxing on the pontoon. One year we found really big snails on the size of a tasty appetizer at a gourmet restaurant. I had never observed them in the 20 years that we have been coming to the lake. "Escargot anyone?"

For some people the "Sand Bar" has other attractions. Boats and pontoons tie up to and turn it into a, well, floating party barge.

For many boaters, the alcohol flows faster than a cow pissing on a flat rock! (That must be really fast!), It's amazing how boating and drinking seems to be ok to so many people!

These same people would not think about drinking and driving! When you add alcohol to boating at the speed that boats and jet ski's travel and add to the mix that water vehicles do not have brakes like a land vehicle, it can be a very dangerous practice!

Michigan put a law into place that if you are ticketed for drinking and operating a boat, it goes on your driving record. This had helped modify some of the adult imbibing. The key is to have a designated captain or driver for the boat! Remember "Safety first!"

❧

I mentioned earlier that the Fourth of July on the lake is celebrated from May to September. It is truly unbelievable to hear fireworks go off most evenings all summer long. I enjoy fireworks, on the Fourth or even on the weekend of the Fourth! But much before or after the Fourth, it gets old.

On the Fourth of July the lake turns into a competitive fireworks wonderland. I was out last year with Dr. Bob, a friend of mine, and we were dazzled by an immense fireworks display put on by a homeowner on the lake.

Dr. Bob turned to me and said, "How does it feel to have watched in 20 minutes someone set off essentially a year's pay in fireworks?"

The large airborne fireworks are usually bought in Indiana, and smuggled into Michigan because they are cheaper from there.

It's an awesome experience to see thousands of fireworks explode and be reflected on the water! My only concern is of course "Safety First!" there have been some accidents with fireworks over the years, and of course without a permit, it can be illegal. While legal on a holiday weekend, on our lake the season starts in May and continues to October. Too many loud noises on a non-holiday weekend for me.

I have to share with you one of the some unique experiences we have enjoyed living on the lake. Our first winter was melting away; the lake was in transition to spring. The ice had been moaning and cracking trying to resist its "shape shifting" back to water. The ice, looking a murky gray, was disappearing and joyous spring was near! Next to us, our neighbor had a dock that had been left in the water all winter. Under the dock, two otters took up residence. Then we noticed, a lot of little otters! They were very cute and playful.

What Chrissy especially liked was the sound they made. The made a high pitched sound that mimicked a squeaky toy! Imaging watching these little otters swimming, playing and squeaking! What fun! They hung out for a couple of weeks, and then they swam away, never to return! We were sad when they went away, watching them had become one of our favorite activities. We kept a vigilant lookout for them, but to no avail.

One evening we were out on the pontoon with friends, it was on a warm July night and we looked north and observed the Aurora Borealis, the northern lights! It was awesome! It was an eerie feeling to see the shimmering lights off in the distance, but it was a thrill.

One cold winter's day I had the thrill of watching about 14 deer running down the ice right in front of my house! I looked for Santa, but he was nowhere to be found.

Then one year later, Chrissy and I observed a red fox walking down the ice, the colors were striking against the snow-white background! We have spotted eagles, owls, hawks, woodpeckers, and many types of non-predator birds. We have seen box turtles, painted turtles and large snapping turtles. We have caught glimpses of bears and coyotes! And don't forget about the "Snipes!" "Hey Chrissy!" "Who needs "Animal Planet"?

∾

Our lake is the result of three rivers flowing together and being dammed up in the early 1920's. The Wolverine Power Company used the dams to generate electricity. The waters back flowed and the lake was born!

Divers have commented that in the deep water, you can still make out the trees that were submerged at that time. There are roads that are now underwater! Watch out for the stumps that seem to be magnets for the propellers on boats.

There were a series of four dams developed by the Wolverine Power Company. This created beautiful lakes that have thousands of homes and cottages.

They provide recreation, tax dollars and an economic infusion of cash that varies by the season.

Many of the lakes in Michigan have been unfortunately introduced to the European milfoil weed that can choke up the waterways for swimming and boating.

Additionally the Zebra Muscles, a small one-inch mollusk, has also moved into the lake. They attach themselves to anything in the water. They also clear up the water by filtering one liter of water per day and consume the algae.

This clearing of the water lets more sunshine penetrate deeper and the weeds grow faster. So like many Michigan lakes, the water is treated to control the nuisance aquatic weeds. I often wonder what the land and waterways must have looked like before all the development, the people and machinery moved in. On the other hand, we human beings are a part of nature, are we not?

An interesting aspect of our lake is to note that in several areas, believe it or not, some brilliant engineer decided to run the electric wires for our power grid, right across the lake! This makes it very interesting for people that decide to go parasailing and sail boating, if the mast is too high it makes for an interesting voyage, as you pass underneath the power lines. I prefer the pontoon, you travel under the power lines and you are glad that you don't have to deal with a tall mast!

The attraction for this lake is the ability to boat for hours at a time, going up different branches of the river and cruising up and down the many different cuts or channels. (This is why our pontoon has a porta potty on it!) The kids just love it when you anchor the pontoon in the deep water and they can dive off the front of the pontoon and climb up the ladder and do it again! This, we have found is a great way to tire kids out!

Of course Chloe, our golden, has to get in the act and jump off the pontoon to be near Chrissy! Chloe, Princess and Buffalo all have their own life jacket's (Safety First). Chloe and Princess have become quite adept at climbing on to a water float to rest!

There are people that feel very passionate about the lake life, spending time outdoors, in the water, on the water, fishing, and hunting and cooking outdoors.

There are also people who prefer to spend their time in hotels with room service, swimming in pools, shopping and taking in dinner and a movie. Both of those lifestyles are awesome, but as for me, I'll see you on the lake!

6 RANCH LIFE

Ranch & farm life in the movies or on television looks pretty relaxing, low key and laid back. People seem always down to earth, land rich and cash poor. Well there is some of that, but it is also a life filled with worry, anxiety, a lot of down right hard work and personal risk both financial and physical!

I truly believe, that it is critically important to give recognition to the farmers, ranchers and all agricultural producers. These are the unsung heroes who spend their lives working day after day bringing food, beverages, clothing and recreation to all of the peoples of the world!

Agricultural workers are at great risk on a daily basis. The Farm Equipment Accident Statistics in the United States, March 31, 2009 states that there are over 120,000 farm worker injuries per year, resulting in over 1,300 fatalities.

Just think about your life! Coffee in the morning, with cream. Cereal for breakfast with milk, toast and butter. A piece of gum on the way to work, cigarettes or chewing tobacco for some. A sandwich with soup or salad for lunch. Dinner might include some wine, vegetables, potato, meat or fish, bread, a piece of pie, ice cream for desert. Wearing a cotton shirt and shorts in the summer, a nice wool hat to go out in the winter. Out for a movie having some popcorn, candy and beverage.

All of this is brought to you by the growers and producers!

Since you have read thus far, you know that we maintain a 50-acre horse ranch. We commercially farm about 38 acres. We rotate crops from hay to corn to winter wheat to soybeans. I'm proud to be involved in this honorable endeavor on a very small scale.

Working on a farm, ranch, orchard, or vineyard is not a 9 to 5 commitment. You give whatever it takes to keep up with your animals, crops and products. Planting and harvest time do not wait! Mother nature is not always agreeable. The seasons continue to change. The cows need milking; the horses need clean stalls, feed and water. The commitment is great! The commitment is 24/7! The work can be physical, but the key is that it is continuous, unforgiving and relentless.

The work can also be very fulfilling. It produces a sense of pride with your product or service. A sense of accomplishment certainly comes at harvest time, but also in the daily accomplishments of your work. Clean fresh stalls; swept aisle ways always give you a sense of accomplishment and pride in your work.

I absolutely love the beauty of the sunsets in the evening and the sunrises in the mornings. No brush to canvas, no photo image can capture the breathtaking vistas, views, light shows and pallet of colors that God paints on the canvass of the earth's skies.

I feel the sense of exhilaration and excitement of the horses as I watch them explode with energy as they head out into the pastures, the thundering of their hooves, the sheer elegance of seeing them buck and rear high up in a "Lipizzaner Stallion" like acrobatic feat!

Even horses have an individual personality. Learning to understand them and working with them using natural horsemanship methods develops a bond, a working relationship based on leadership, trust and time spent with your animal.

It is an incredible feeling watching a seed germinate and begin showing the shoots of life beginning to reach for the sky and the life giving sun! Over time, these shoots grow tall and develop into a plant that can be harvested.

The seasons, while are each very different, all have their positives and negatives. As I'm writing this book it is winter. Winter can be very devastating for stock and wildlife animals. Winter brings with it bitter bone chilling cold, the freezing temperatures, the drifting of snow covering food sources, there is ice that may cause dangerous slipping, falling and tripping. It seems every year a horse or two in our community has to be put down from a tragic fall. There are the grey days with the lack of sunshine that may cause depression or just the blue feelings.

Winter also has its advantages, no flies, mosquitoes or other insects. I love the crunching sound of walking on the snow on a sub-zero day. I love the glistening look of crystal chandeliers, when you look at the trees after an ice storm on a sunny day. In Michigan there is generally very little rain (except in ice storms!), lightning (on occasion), or tornadoes in winter.

And I really like my Ferrier, but I have to admit, fewer visits in the winter are a financial benefit!

The Ferrier is the person who comes to your barn and for a fee will trim your horse's hooves and put horseshoes on them if appropriate. The hooves grow slower in the winter months, so you have fewer visits by the Ferrier. Also the horses grow thick, bushy, winter coats. It keeps them warm, but they lose their shiny summer look under all of that hair.

Spring blooms with all of its freshness and its renewal of life! A transition from winter to summer! A virtual rebirth with the budding of the trees, plants slowly reaching for the sky, the birds returning from down south, animals emerging from hibernation, and insects to make the season more interesting. The greening up of the grasses and trees, the sounds of spring, the water in a stream running swollen with the spring melt. The sounds of wings beating overhead as the geese and ducks return from their southern adventures.

With the spring, then comes the rains, thunder and lightning, and yes mud! Our property has some sand, but mostly it is topsoil clay. You slip on your mud boots, and slide out, sometimes sinking in over you ankles, sometimes up to your knees! At times the mud is so coagulated, that it will suck your boots right off your feet! What a feeling it is to realizes that you are slopping barefoot in the cold mucky mud. Inevitably, you will misstep and land on your butt, in the mud! If you are observed as this act occurs, laughter will follow.

Summer for the inhabitants of the northern states, is a time of joy, (Although we do have a lot of Christmas in July parties!) Michiganders truly love summer! No winter coats, hats, gloves, boots or frostbite! We long for the day when the warm breezes finally embrace Michigan. Then we are off swimming, boating! Riding in a T-Shirt, golfing, baseball, soccer, tennis, and anything outdoors! There are local festivals every weekend in Michigan. We have cherry festivals, maple syrup festivals, medieval festivals, beer, fishing, speed boating, art, rib, burger and even potato festivals.

With the summer comes the bugs, biting flies, sunburn's, stinging bees, hornets, wasps and summer heat. Summer heat, mixed with high humidity means oppressively high heat indexes, and sweating!

It seems that you just get done cutting the lawn, pastures, front of property and weed whacking and it's time to start cutting the lawn, pastures, front of property and weed whacking again!

The manure ripens and urine magically changes it to ammonia.

"What's up with that?"

We need to take a moment and discuss the manure spreader. The manure spreader is an important part of agriculture. Essentially, you fill the spreader with manure. The spreader varies in length and width; depending on how many animals you are spreading for. The one we use, attaches to the tractor and when you pull it down the field, the gears are connected to the spinners toward the back of the machine and the bed that moves the manure forward. The result is the manure is pushed and slung out over a wide area behind the spreader. It will break down and make excellent nutrients for the crops.

Fall brings out a beautiful pallet of colors in the Midwest as the trees burnout for another year! Amazing colors, brilliant reds, yellows, browns, and seemingly all colors are on display. The colors are breathtaking, brilliant, subdued and glorious. The challenge is to determine the best time to see the "Peak Color Tour!" It is announced nightly on many newscasts, as it a tremendous tourist attraction, and that means a boon to the economy in Michigan.

I love the smells of fall, like the burning of leaves, cooking potatoes wrapped in foil and buried in the burning freshly raked makeshift oven. There are moist and musty grassy, moldy and earthy smells. Fall is a time of transition, a reflection of summer festivities. Apple cider, donuts and Halloween and more festivals! Festivals like October fest, or the Bavarian fest! And they lead of course to a plethora of "winter festivals!"

Fall is the "Baton down the Hatches" prepatory season to get ready for winter. All of the hay, feed and horse waterers need to be ready for the winter blasts. Fall is filled with illusions. One day its is gray and 38 degrees and the next day its 72 degrees and sunny. Often the mud returns with the cold rains!

Each of the seasons has its attractions and detractions. And every one at the "Woof & Whinny Ranch," has their favorites, their likes and their dislikes. But one thing is constant with the changes of the season, the chores are there, daily chores must get done, no matter how long they take. Ownership of animals, crops, orchards all producers require a total commitment from the individual's and their families.

As for me - 'I Love Summer!"

I have to admit that I'm having a personal relationship with my tractor. Who would have ever thought? After all I was a city boy who dreamed of having a Jaguar or Porsche to drive around the city streets during my mid-life crisis. I have to admit that it feels great when I climb aboard my "New Holland Boomer Series" tractor.

There is a book that will help explain this relationship, it's called "Old Tractors and the Men Who Love Them" (and don't forget the beloved companion book;

"Old Long Johns and the Men Who Wear Them" - just kidding!)

The tractor on a ranch or farm is a critical work tool. There are so many tasks that tractors perform. Tractors save time, energy, backs and muscles. Tractors are used for moving and lifting heavy objects that are impossible to do with manpower alone.

Over the years I have come to understand how the tractor has helped to elevate the agricultural industry to the height's it has reached today. I have observed the Amish, working the fields, haying, harvesting with horse and manpower. This is a very time and labor intense process.

Moving round bales with the tractor is an easy task, spreading manure, hauling water, plowing the snow, building an access road, and brush hogging a pasture. All of these tasks I have done with my tractor.

If you have a chance this summer, look up your local fly wheelers or antique tractor association, and attend a tractor show. You will find this very educational and fun to see a steam tractor in action. Attend a tractor pull the competition you will witness, is raw power in action.

Ranch life is a life long learning experience. I'm at the very beginner level of horseback riding. I'm a little unsure of my self and of the horse. I have a tough time getting on and off the horse, it's more of a mental block that a physical one. I hope to improve my skills and confidence, to really enjoy riding.

My first horse was not very helpful in that regard. He was a big black horse called "Fury." He was fun to be around, always came up for a treat or to just hang out with you.

I remember the day I went to ride him. I climbed up and I accidently kicked him in the side on my way up. Kicking a horse on your way to mount him is not the best thing to do, Fury immediately began to buck, I lasted 5 times and then I swung my leg over and was bucked off into the air! I landed on the hard snow in the arena area, and the bruise was a royal looking black and blue. (Where is the video camera when you need it!)

It really did hurt, my pride, and my rear where I landed. Fury of course looked on with a sense of pride in what he had accomplished, or so it looked!

What I want to share with you is that if you are not an experienced rider, stay away from horses named "Fury", "Diablo", "Thunder" or "Widow Maker"!

The next horse I bought and rode was a Halflinger named "Daisy." Daisy and I quickly bonded. Daisy likes to eat, walk, eat, roll in the field and did I mention eat?

When I first met Daisy she reminded me of a middle-aged housewife who is always in the kitchen baking cakes, cookies, pies, lasagna, casseroles, muffins, and more cakes! You know the type, they smile all the time and usually wear one of several "Hawaiian muumuus" that they have in their closets next to the sweat pants. They are still wondering just what is Victoria's Secret!

Daisy's previous owner had kept her in the pasture 24/7. This presented with two problems for Daisy; first she was able to eat 24/7 and did! Second there was a bull in the field and he kept attempting to mate with her (bulls and teenage boys seem to have a lot in common). Daisy seemed happy to be going home to the ranch with us.

Chrissy did a "Safety first" test for Daisy, she stood up on Daisy's back with her arms spread out and Daisy just stood there! Chrissy approved Daisy as "Daddy Safe!"

Life on the ranch includes injuries, death, taxes, feed, and veterinarian bills! If you own horses, you will become very familiar with your vet.

I want to share with you one of the most difficult injuries we have had to deal with. Envy is one of our "Paints". Envy is a special horse, anyone can ride her, and she has the temperament of a saint. She's steady, calm and always working with her, as the renowned horse trainer Parreli would say "right brain!"

Envy was in her paddock one day, and somehow she managed to get her leg tangled in the soft white vinyl fence wire. The vinyl should have broke when she pulled on it, but unfortunately, it didn't.

We don't know how long she was caught in this predicament. When Chrissy, Carol and one of Christy's friends went to the barn to do chores, they found Envy, and called for help. Carol cut the vinyl wire and freed up Envy, but the damage was already done.

Farm calls are expensive, $120.00 just for the vet to walk on the property, and the price seems to go up monthly. Envy could not be trailered, so this service was needed.

The vet examined Envy and the news was not good. She had cut off the circulation so long, essentially cutting off the blood supply similar to a tourniquet, that she was going to lose some part of her hoof.

A horse has five hearts, the cardiovascular heart and its four hooves. A horse needs all five to survive.

Her prescription included soaking of the hoof and leg in warm saltwater twice a day, and bandaging it up with a diaper and vet wrap.

Vet wrap is an ingenious material that when applied and wrapped back on itself will hold together like duct tape, but vet wrap does not have any adhesive glue on it! We bought cases of vet wrap!

This was to be done twice a day for months if she was going to have a chance to regrow the cap or hoof. There of course were anti-inflammatory medications, antibiotics and pain medications. The vet was not certain that this would work, but it was her only chance, and we were committed to saving her. She deserved this chance.

I have to give full credit to Carol and Chrissy, they went to work and kept on nursing Envy for month after month. After about 6 months, she went in for an x-ray, and to everyones excitement, the part of the hoof that was damaged, began growing back! We rejoiced at the news.

There were still issues; the hoof was not growing back correctly and there was a proud flesh area that would prove to be a long process to heal. But now she had a chance.

The vet said that 90% of the horse owners would not have put in the constant effort of soaking and bandaging to bring Envy through this crisis. Hats off to Carol and Chrissy. I did help on weekends, but I played a small part in her recovery.

It took a couple of years and Envy was doing better, but still not walking properly and having proudflesh issues. It took special intervention by Envy's previous owner who owns a hydrotherapy business specializing in horse injury rehabilitation. She brought her $50,000+ dollar machine to our stable and taught us how to run it for two weeks of therapy.

The next step was to bring Envy to her location and have a twice a day intensive therapy applied, she did all of this at her own expense. Envy indeed is a special horse!

She also worked with an expert Ferrier, who was able to study the x-rays and develop a plan to trim the hoof, a little at a time to bring its shape back as close as possible.

All of these efforts payed off! Envy is now walking properly and able to go trail riding! She loves running in the pasture, and playing with the other horses. Life is good again for Envy!

Thank you to our vet, Envy's previous owner, her partner, Carol and Chrissy, and everyone else who participated in Envy's recovery.

∾

Let's talk manure! Yes I have indeed spread a lot of manure in the last few years! Politicians, it is said, may be guilty of the same thing! As a city boy, it is amazing to learn how much manure a horse can generate in one day! It reminds me of a trip to Mackinac Island, Michigan. If you have not spent some time there, put it on your "Bucket List"!

You can spend days on Mackinac Island! There is a lot to do and see. The walk or bike ride around the island is a little over eight miles. It has some of the most beautiful shoreline views anywhere in the world!

The scenery is always changing, different sides of the island offer different views; other islands, the Michigan's upper peninsula, the "Mighty Mac" bridge, and the scene of the boats ferrying people from the mainland. The town itself is a collage of many shops, resteraunts, historical sites, hotels, bed & breakfast's, and of course, the fudge shops!

(That's where the nickname of "fudgies" came from!) Every one it seems has a favorite shop. The fudge varies in flavors; is very rich, delicious and addicting. A little taste is all you need. Although I did have a friend of mine purchase five pounds of the tasty fudge in various flavors to bring back home for family and friends. Unfortunately over the weekend he consumed all five pounds, and had to purchase more fudge to bring home. I don't know if it's a record to consume that much, but it should be. I really don't know how he did it!

There are no autos on the island, except for an emergency ambulance. If you have seen the movie "Somewhere in Time" with Jane Seymour and Christopher Reeves, you will be familiar with the island.

In the movie Christopher drove a car on the island, that's the only way to see an automobile on Mackinac Island, they are forbidden.

Most people bike around the island. You can take horse driven taxis, and tours. You can rent a horse and buggy and drive it yourself or you can even rent a horse to ride around the island.

However you get around, somewhere in the center of the island is a huge, gigantic, mammoth, extra large, Grande, mountain sized manure pile! It will be composted and used right on the island. There is an inexhaustible supply of manure. There are full time workers who simply go up and down the streets, sweeping up the manure and depositing it in their carts.

There is nothing like Mackinac Island in the summer. On a hot day the dense aroma wafts through the air, the throngs of vacationers generate a blend of fudge, horse manure, sweat, and coconut suntan lotion! What fun!

My family particularly enjoys going in the fall, the days are usually crisp and cool, great for walking and biking! When Chrissy was five and each trip since then, whenever we would take a horse drawn taxi or tour, she would relentlessly ask the driver if she could take over the reins.

She would be very persistent, and then due to the kindness of the drivers, and the fact that she was taking riding lessons, in a less traveled area of the trip they would let her drive the horses! She loved it!

Mackinac Island offers many overnight accommodations, several hotels and bed & breakfast spots. This is a destination that is indeed "Somewhere in Time"!

∽

During the winter months at the ranch, you cannot spread the manure in the fields due to the amount of snow. The ranch pile does not rival Mackinac Islands "Manure Mountain", but in the spring it can take 8 to 15 hours to scoop it up and spread the manure in the fields.

Farms and ranches deal with a lot of manure. All animals generate some kind of excrement that must be dealt with in an environmentally acceptable way. And they do!

I'm reminded of a trip to the county fair. My dad and I went into the cow barn to look at, well the cows! My dad noticed that there were two teenage girls tending to the cows. They were walking in amongst them. And they were bare foot! Now this upset my dad, and he asked one of the girls if they minded being barefoot walking around the cows and of course the manure.

The young girl answered "I don't mind it at all, its warm and squishy, and my feet are a lot easier to clean than my tennis shoes!"

The logic was right on, but dad just couldn't get over the bare feet!

The ranch property is set up with the riding arena, stable and tractor barn at the front of the property. Next are the fields that are commercially farmed. Behind the fields is an area that is full of trees and paths. There is a ridge that drops down about 40 ft into a cedar swamp. Running through the swamp area is a small stream. It is really beautiful and restful to go back there.

The topography buffers the sounds from the road and mostly you hear the forest sounds. A beekeeper worked his hives for years in an opening amongst the trees. With the honey, there was a problem with bears. The beekeeper would lose one or two hives a season. He even tried to put up a solar powered electric fence to keep the bears out, but to no avail. He finally gave up and packed up the rest of the hives and left. We will miss the beautiful honey that the hives produced.

The ranch has lots of wildlife, raccoons, foxes, bobcats, squirrels, deer, woodcock, occasional turkey, pheasants and deer. I mention occasional because when I go out to hunt them in their appropriate season, they seem to disappear. It's like they know! Really, I've gone back there and have almost been run over by a deer, (grandma's not allowed to go back there near Christmas, just in case).

When I go back to hunt deer, nada, zip, zero, nothing! Not hide, nor hair! The deer must be connected on line or like the animals in the movie "Avatar" mother earth warns them. Oh well, I just love to be in the great outdoors, even if its just to watch the sunrise and sunsets.

∾

Hey! I mean hay! If you have horses, you must have hay! And a lot of it! As spring dissolves into summer, the hay grows and before you know it its time to cut the hay, and then bale the hay. Doesn't that sound like fun?

There really is a bit of luck involved in haying. You are so dependent on the weather. The key issue is rain.

The hay must be on the dry side to cut. Once cut it needs to sit in the field for a short period of time to dry out. If it rains while it is drying in the field you have to wait some more.

Why is this so important? Wet hay can mold - not a good thing to feed to horses. If you stack wet hay bales in your barn, believe it or not, they generate methane gas and can spontaneously catch on fire and burn your barn down. Life in the country has its dangers just like life in the city.

One thing I don't understand is why, when it comes to offloading the bales of hay from the hay wagon, it always seem to time out to be the hottest, muggiest, sweatiest, nights of the summer. I'm not kidding! You get drenched in sweat!

You drink gallons of water, but when you are throwing 45 pound bales up to the stacker who places them one way and then the other way to balance the stacks, its hot!

You can't work in a t-shirt and shorts because of hay burn a rash that can appear on your skin. No kidding, the hay is just sharp enough that if you lean into it or drag it across your skin when throwing or stacking, you get red bumps, or even red bleeding bumps and it really stings!

Now granted that if you are 18 or 19 this takes a little effort and then you're done and you head out to the "Corner House" for a double or a "Pig's Platter" ice cream. If you eat it all and get your name posted on the wall for all to see!

Chrissy ate one once and her name will live in infamy at the "Corner House".

But for those of us over 55, when you're done, a quick flop in the lake to cool off and to get rid of the hay dust feels awesome!

Now normally, we put up (stack) about 350 bales of hay. Many ranches and farms put up 1200 to 2000+ bales.

That takes a lot of time and effort! But it has to be done!

Round bales are easier to deal with in regard to stacking. You use the tractor and stack them up! Round bales are great in the winter, just pop'em into a feeder and the horses have at it!

Round bales are just too difficult to feed the horses in the stable environment. Square bales are best; you can determine the correct number of flakes of hay for each horse.

∽

Now if you have horses you must have a tack room. The tack room has all of the items to be able to saddle and ride your horse, as well as to extract large sums of money from the horse owner.

Chrissy has a lot of saddles! It's like living with someone in a TV episode of "Hoarders" We have more saddles than we have horses! We have multiples of the same type of saddle!

The list of tack is endless; Halters, reins, boots, cinches, medical boots for horses to work in, rehabilitate in and trailer in. We have lead ropes, spurs, and whips, lunge lines, combs, brushes, picks, massagers (for the horses). We have blankets of all sizes, fly masks, fly sheets, saddle pads, saddle blankets, chaps, hats and helmets, assorted pins and on and on!

Next is the feed room! We have sweet feed, safe feed, beet pulp; supplements to help put weight on, supplements to help take weight off!

Supplements to strengthen their hoofs, bones and joints! Supplements for a shiny coat! Honestly it's like walking into a General Nutrition Center for Horses!

Next are the medical supplies, I mentioned vet wrap but it doesn't stop there. We have wormer, cool pack jell, lots of ointments and balms for; eye, skin, muscle aches, bites, stings, scratches and cuts. We have "bute" a super painkiller, injectables, and a horseshoe hanging up for good luck! We even have little bugs shipped in monthly that attack and kill the fly larva.

The office in the barn is nicely appointed. All my life I collected painted saws but I never knew why. I never had a place to hang them, but I still collected them over the years. Now they hang proudly on the walls of the office. They look like they are meant to there. There are deer scenes, pheasant scenes and farm scenes painted on them.

Chrissy also has her wall of fame. She has many of her awards, and ribbons that she has earned over the years. It looks great!

We also have lots of art, some painted from talented friends and a cool wooden duck carving from brother Doug, the wood carver!

The bathroom with shower comes in handy as does the stove and refrigerator for the days that we spend a lot of time at the ranch. It is also furnished with black leather couches that are futons for sleeping overnight.

And don't forget the barn cats. We have two rescue cats. "Angel" is a gorgeous calico cat. Her colors are stunning! Her temperament is very loving, as long as you are willing to pet her for significant periods of time.

When we called the rescue, the people were concerned about letting us have her because she was to live in a stable. We invited them over to see kitty's accommodations first hand. We showed them the warm room, a heated room the cats can access through a kitty door and then the office. One of them commented that they could be happy living in the office and that kitty would be happy living at the stable. We adopted her and she is in her 5th year with us.

We have another rescue cat "Keylie," a black and white kitty with an unusual face. Chrissy found Keylie while she was working part time at a vet office in town.

The vet was kind enough to spay Keylie if Chrissy (meaning us) would adopt her. And so we did! Both cats add a lot to the stable and of course are excellent mousers.

Before becoming a cat owner, I did not realize how much cats love to be petted and how loud they purr, it's really nifty! Yes it's true, dogs may have owners, cats have staff.

The ranch has been an expense to operate, and a lot of work. Most importantly the ranch has been a therapeutic respite, from our busy hectic modern life.

We love spending time with the horses, grooming them, being around them and for Chrissy enjoying the exhilaration of the competition, and the special bond with her horses, has made it all well worthwhile!

One fact it seems for many horse owners is that you don't always keep horses forever. There is a lot of horse trading, buying selling, and in tough economic times, horse giving!

We were feeling a little horse heavy, with cutbacks at my company coming up, and were looking to sell a couple of horses. Our horse friends from Muskegon called and let us know that there was a riding instructor looking for an older, calm and gentle horse for training younger children the basics of riding. She felt that Honey, our oldest horse, would be a good fit. She had observed Chrissy riding Honey at a fun horse show competition.

The thought of Honey getting all of the love and attention of children just beginning in their equestrian lives sounded like a wonderful way for Honey to spend the twilight of her career.

Honey was a great horse. Let me share an example of her ability to stay calm. We live about 45 minutes south of a National Guard camp. We also happen to have a dam at one end of the lake.

Sometimes in the summer at our lake, military jet planes will practice their skills by swooping down at tree top level, and take a pretend shot at the dam.

Imagine this, Chrissy and Carol had brought Honey home to ride around the neiborhood. Some friends came over to see Honey with their 4-year-old daughter. She just couldn't wait to get up on Honey!

All of a sudden a jet swooped down a tree top level. This was very loud and caused all of us to jump or move when the sound pierced the air. Honey, just stood there with the child on her back and did not move or flinch! Wow!

It could have been a very dangerous situation had Honey bolted with the child on her back! What a great and gentle horse Honey is!

So I contacted the instructor, described Honey and the fact that our mutual contact in Muskegon recommended Honey for the job, and it was a go! He wanted Honey!

He asked how much money we wanted for Honey, but we were so pleased and thrilled to find such a perfect home for her that we told him that we just wanted a good home for Honey! So we set a date and off we went to deliver Honey to her new home in Indiana!

We wanted to make this a one-day trip, so we started off early. We put the other horses out in the pastures and loaded up Honey for her journey. The other horses are always paying attention whenever you drive off with a member of the herd! They looked anxiously at the trailer, as we pulled out of the ranch.

We began our journey and at first it was very uneventful. Our Ford F-250 Super Duty diesel pulls the trainer with ease. After about two hours, we stopped at a rest area and Carol took over driving.

After about an hour, we were getting low on fuel and decided to stop into a service station to get some diesel. As Carol attempted to drive around to the other side of the station, we heard a loud noise and the truck stopped in a lurching and shaking move! Not good!

Carol had misjudged the turn and hit the steel and cement posts that protect the gas pumps. They worked, as they protected the gas pumps, but they did not protect our trailer!

The fender was hit and pushed into the wheel causing a flat and bending the actual wheel! Not Good! We later learned that it had bent the axel about one inch.

So there we were, stuck in a service station off the expressway with a very nervous horse in the trailer!

I would not have wanted my blood pressure checked, but I was able to keep my temper in check, as after all accidents do happen.

In reflection, it probably was not the best idea to let Carol drive as she was scheduled for cataract surgery! I felt that I should have known better.

We took Honey out and walked her along a grassy area that was located beside the service station. The people at the service station were really great about the situation. We called our insurance company and they set up a tire service to come out and fix the tire. I told them the wheel was damaged, but of course no one told the repairman.

The waiting was agony, Chinese water torture, or water boarding, or pulling out your fingernails, chalkboard screeching, are we there yet tortuous waiting! The entire process took about five hours off our schedule!

Then we were back on the road! We arrived at Honey's new home around dusk, but there was still enough light out to see a beautiful horse ranch! I felt like we had arrived at "Tara" from "Gone With The Wind"! The main house was very new, and the property seemed to sprawl forever! There appeared to be two stables connected to an indoor riding arena.

We took pictures for Chrissy and drove up to meet Honey's new owner. We were thrilled with the hospitality, the personal style, the stall, stable, riding arena and absolutely everything about Honey's new home!

It made the drive back, with me as the only driver, and remember five hours behind schedule, all worthwhile!

One additional bonus about having horses, taking care of them and the ranch work for kids growing up, is that it takes a lot of time, discipline and love for the animals. Chrissy made the point that it didn't leave her with a lot of time on her hands to get in trouble while growing up!

7 HIGH SCHOOL YEARS

One key issue that was noticeably different when Chrissy began high school was the passage of time. It seemed to go faster each year! Added to that, she wanted to be called Chris. An accomidation that I became used to.

I thought about this phenomenon and I recalled some comments from my grandfather, "Years seem like months, months seem like weeks, weeks seem like days and days seem like hours, time goes faster as you get older!"

I have to agree, as I'm getting older time does indeed seem to be going faster. I remember when I was in high school sitting in study hall for a 45 minute block of time. I remember how endless time seemed until it the bell rang and it was time leave. I would do all my homework, read a few chapters in a book and look up at the clock and to my dismay 15 minutes went by. Wow! That seemed like an eternity until that bell rang and I could go to my next class. Of course today, 45 minutes breezes right on by, hardly noticeable at all.

So, it came to pass, Chris began 9th grade. High School is a real time of transition in so many ways and on so many levels. High School is a time to stretch your wings, test the limits that are put upon you and to determine who you are, and what the goals are you want to set for yourself.

High School a time to focus on your academics, on sports, theatre, music and plays. All of these are fun and great developmental activities. The challenge is that these activities are set against the backdrop of peer pressure, cliques, dating, and sexual experimentation.

To make matters more challenging it is all mixed in with the availability of drugs and alcohol. Freshman seem so young and inexperienced, fortunately parents still have some impact and control on what they can do. The freshman year is filled with new experiences, new friends, and an increasing awareness that there is a lot of adult behavior going on. For many it is very enticing.

Sophomores have an idea of what's going on, but for many reasons they just don't totally get it! With good parental control, they do not have the means to participate in all that is available to them. If they are left on their own, with no curfews and a pocketful of money, situations may occur. This seems to be the beginnings of serious push back against their parents. An attitude almost the same as when they were two, the terrible teen years begin.

Juniors often have their own transportation, stay out later and know what's going on. They test the waters. At this point, parenting groundwork comes to be tested! As parents you have to hope that all the efforts you made earlier in their lives will pay dividends.

Parents still have some control with curfews, car keys that can be taken away, and restriction of allowance.

Seniors believe that they know everything and can do anything. And many of them do. They feel that they are mature adults, and think they should have access to everything adults have. Unfortunately, many of them are not ready emotionally or financially for adulthood.

Mistakes can be made when children and young adults enter into non-age appropriate adult behavior. This includes behaviors that are sampled before they are both physically and mentally ready. There are physical acts that kids engage in that result in negative outcomes, if they are not financially and emotionally mature enough to handle the unintended consequences. My heart goes out to parents that have to deal with these circumstances.

We see these situations all the time, underage pregnancies and the increase in the welfare rolls. The challenge with this circumstance, in addition to taxing the welfare rolls, often sets the stage for the inability for the young women to reach their full potential. They may miss their opportunity to develop their gifts and interests that may have led them to a satisfying career and a parenting situation that may have benefited both mother and the planned for child.

Substance abuse can be devastating at any age, but for developing children and young adults, it can lower their self-image, grade point and ultimate ability to reach their potential. Parents need to set a good example in this regards. Remember young adults may lack impulse control, it seems to develop sometime in their twenty's.

And all of this occurs with music in the background that parents usually cannot tolerate! It's usually played too loud! (According to the parents!) My daughter says it is just another example of being too old. One thing is for certain, as a parent that went to High School years ago, I'm glad that I'm not going through it now! We were allowed to be kids for a while instead of having to act like an adult!

Most parents only want to help their children make the right choices, and to do the right thing. It's the push back and the testing that teenagers do that can get things out of control.

Another example of episodic insanity, and it applies both for parents and for teenagers. I have witnessed some parents act like their kids best buddy, and let them do pretty much whatever they want. I have observed some parents take themselves out of the situation and let their kids experiment with no boundaries, or curfews. And I have also observed parents exert so much control; they lose their children to complete rebellion. What's the answer? Let me know if you find out!

Yep, when I was with Chris and met some of her friends and friend's parents, I was jokingly always introduced as her "ATM and Chauffer"! But really it was no joke! I was ok with it, that is the role of a parent at that stage of development.

High School for Chris was a great opportunity to reach out and experience life in many directions. Being in a small school system has disadvantages and advantages. Less competition leads to more opportunities to be involved in several directions.

High School for many young adults begins the "dating" or "going out" years. Indeed, kids start going out with someone before they can literally go out. They do not go anywhere, but they can still go out with someone. Reflecting back to 7th and 8th grades, there was a going out theme, but it did not have any real meaning. In High School, it does.

For some lucky parents this begins in college or after High School. Some parents prohibit dating in high school, but watch out when the kids go away to college!

Chris to my dismay at times and delight at other times has been interested in the opposite sex since grade school. This is an affliction that I also was under the influence of as I grew up, so I have some empathy. It has resulted in a significant lack of sleep in my life.

The lack of sleep was usually due to staying awake, and dreaming about the relationships until the wee hours of the night.

From grade school on, Chris generally had a boyfriend. Out of respect for Chris's privacy and her boyfriends, I'm not going to deal with specifics. I do however want to share some general situations.

How cute it is to see friendship relationships develop with very young children. They take turns coming over to each other's homes for supervised playtime. They usually dine on macaroni and cheese, spaghettios, grilled cheese or hot dogs. It is fun to see kids play and get along so well. This is all about their social development.

As grade school gives way to middle school, the cuteness is still alive and well. Now of course it's bowling together, rollerblading together, going to movies all with adult supervision. Birthday parties are a mandatory social event. Parents are usually ok with these types of activities.

When High School starts, the cuteness has long worn off of these budding relationships. Parents are now concerned with all of the challenges of non-age appropriate behaviors. Parents initiate curfews, investigate supervision at parties, sleepovers and other types of teen gatherings.

Yes at times it seems like you are playing detectives like "Mike Hammer", "Magnum PI", "Rockford" or even "Dragnet". "Just the facts, ma'am".

∽

Let's consider today's electronic age. First, cell phones and the teenager. At first I was reluctant to obtain a cell phone for Chris. I thought to myself, "Why in the world would a teenager need a cell phone?"

I had observed other teenagers mindlessly chatting on their phones as they walked, rode bikes or were just shopping. I'm sure the discussions were intellectually stimulating.

What sold me on the idea of getting Chris a cell phone was in her freshman year she was coming back late one night from a game. I remember sitting listening to satellite radio for an hour. It occurred to me that if she had a phone, she could have called me at home with an ETA. Also if she was at a teenage gathering, and wanted to go home early, she could just call me. I liked that idea, and she got her phone.

What did we do before cell phones became available? We used to leave messages for people where we thought they were going to be. We would plan in advance. We would leave written notes. We were dazzled with he invention of the beeper. Then came the old bag phones that were too bulky and used too much power to carry around.

The original cell phones were large really huge, you almost needed a backpack to carry them! I remember the "Dick Tracy" newspaper cartoons featuring the wristwatch communicator. Who would have believed that it's a reality today! My only suggestion, is to make sure you have unlimited calls, text and Internet access, or the charges can add up quickly.

A recent story in the news was about a teenage boy who text a friend internationally and ran up a $22,000.00 texting bill. That might deplete the college savings!

Of course in the future, there may be a one charge all inclusive communications bill that is individualized and applies to the communications implant in your head!

And of course the World Wide Web can be very dangerous, with access to adult sites and undesirable people trying to get connected with kids for horrific reasons. Then there is Facebook and Twitter. It is critical for parents to monitor these activities.

∽

When Chris was in the 8th grade, she tried out for a play and won a singing part for the song "Anything You Can Do, I Can Do Better." She loved doing it and her partner in the duet was also very talented. She loved the experience and was in many plays during high school.

In her freshman year she joined the cheerleader club for football. She is very enthusiastic, high energy and loved cheerleading. I attended all of the home games and went on the road to many more. It was fun to watch her cheering skills develop.

In central Michigan, the weather can change at a moments notice. The saying goes "If you don't like the weather, wait ten minutes it will probably change." While attending a football game the weather can change from sunny and 60 degrees to sleeting and 35 degrees from kick off to last down. Wearing layers of clothing, rain gear and a soft stadium seat pad can be a wonderful thing on game night!

Dad the ATM or money machine was operating at all games. Dad would provide hot chocolate, water and popcorn on the cold nights, and cold pop, water and a hot dog on the warm nights. I was happy to attend, I enjoyed the games, watching Chris and of course I enjoyed the hot chocolate!

There is still something exhilarating about a crisp fall night when the ball is in play, the band is playing, and the cheerleaders are pumping up the crowd. It just plain feels good! I loved attending the games and I still do!

We are also blessed with a fantastic music teacher at our school. She is very gifted at getting the best out of her students.

She works them very hard, winning lots of competitions, all while receiving their gratitude, love and respect. Chris enjoyed all four of her years spent in choirs. She also volunteered to cantor at church services, then she volunteered me to cantor and I still enjoy cantoring to this day!

The first of the high school trips began. These trips are a great opportunity for kids to get away from their communities and see more of the world. The first of these trips was to Cedar Point, Ohio.

Cedar Point's theme is the roller coaster capital of the world and it is. The trip consisted of a bus ride down to Cedar Point, an overnight at a hotel, a full day of rides and the trip home! Carol and I in a weak moment of episodic insanity, volunteered to help chaperone the trip. This was also to minimize my suffering from DWAS syndrome (Dad's Worry And Stress Syndrome).

It was interesting that the chaperones at the hotel scheduled an all night vigil; we signed up to monitor the hall in 2-hour shifts. One interesting tactic was that after the kids were in their rooms, we were instructed to tape all around the outside of the doors. If the tape would be pulled off the door, we would know when we walked by that the door was opened and that someone may have left their room. It turned out to be an uneventful night.

The morning began with high excitement and energy.

After breakfast it was off to the park! The look on the kid's faces was awesome! They were with their friends and truly happy. Cedar Point is one of the coolest parks on the planet. Their energy exuded excitement, enthusiasm, and high energy. It looked like they ate "Neutrino's" for breakfast!

We asked the kids to stay in groups as they went through the day and had parents stationed at various sites if assistance was needed. Chris was in her element, speed and action at its best, coaster after coaster!

Carol and I went to roam through the park and occasionally caught glimpses of her and her friends.

When I was younger, I used to love the coasters, but nowadays the park bench was more to my liking and of course the smoked turkey leg was my favorite attraction!

It was a super trip, at the end of the day we all rendezvoused at the bus and the kids were exhausted! The bus took on the unique aroma of 50 plus sweaty tired teenagers and chaperones mixed with cotton candy, sunblock, and the back of the bus porta potty fumes!

There were stuffed animals won on the midway, popcorn, all types of candy and the usual tourist memorabilia to bring home! What Fun!

There would be many more high school trips, some to Cedar Pointe, Los Angeles, New York, Chicago and Florida! We did not chaperone any more trips, but Chris loved all of them, and brought home many memories that she will cherish forever!

The teachers did their best to help kids attend trips with limited means by way of fundraising for trips. I commend them for this. I also must admit that I was a little queasy about sending Chris off to faraway places, but I bucked up and let her spread her wings. I recommend helping your kids to take advantage of all of these types of activities.

Parent involvement with their children's education and extra-curricular activities can result in an exponential payback. Lack of involvement can have very negative consequences. I have to salute the majority of the parents who step up and are there for their kids. I'm always amazed that some parents do not attend the parent teacher conferences. Some do not attend because their kids are doing well, and they don't feel that it is important to go since there are no problems.

The reality is it is important! What a great opportunity to have teachers brag about your child in front of them. It can bolster confidence, build relationships with the teachers and motivate the kids to do even better!

Some parents don't attend because it will be less than a positive experience. Some unfortunately just don't care. This is when teenagers need their parent, or parents to attend, and to learn that their kids are doing many things well. Parents may also learn that there are other things that could be improved on. A little support, compassion, suggestions, and empathy may help turn a situation around.

I understand that at the end of a long workday, filled with the stresses of the job can take its toll. Also for many just the transit to and from work can be exhausting. The weather might be an issue on the night of the conference. The reality is that many parents who do attend are dealing with the same issues. Invest the time, invest in your kids and you may have dividends for semesters or even years to come!

∾

Another fun aspect of the high school years is that they occur smack dab in the middle of hormone changes. Wow, it can be like living with someone with tri-polar disease. I mean it's tough enough living with two human females and three canine females.

I sometimes feel like I'm adrift in a "sea of estrogen"! Between the teenage years of fluctuating hormones and the menopause years with Carol, I sometimes felt like waving the white flag!

I have observed Chris being on an emotional roller coaster with its ups and downs all in the same hour, day or even during a phone conversation. Growing up is a tough thing to go through.

The emotions between getting a boyfriend, breaking up with a boyfriend, being dropped by a boyfriend and plotting to catch a new boyfriend, it's sometimes hard to keep up with the drama!

These teenage relationships can look serious and last a long time or they can be here today and gone tomorrow. I have observed the flavor of the month boyfriend routine! Boyfriends even seem to rotate around from girlfriend to girlfriend, and that's okay as long as the break-up occurs before the rotation. If the switch to another partner occurs before the break-up, then it's called cheating.

One key rule was in place during high school; do not talk about the "guinea pig in the freezer!" Sure enough, it would be discovered by a teenage boy or girl rummaging through the freezer looking for something to eat.

It would start out as a surprised howl, and then a "What the "expletive deleted" is this?" would be shouted out.

This was a great conversation starter when Chris was having a sleepover with her girlfriends. It was awesome; with the girls first you would hear high-pitched "eeek!" And then a low pitch, shuddering "eeeeuuuuuuhhh!" Then the questions came flying at Chris. She always handled them in a matter of fact way, and everyone said that they understood.

82

The next thing you knew it was summer! My absolute favorite season!

I worked as a sales manager, and covered a fair amount of geography. Often I would leave early in the morning, around 6:30 a.m. I would drive for a couple of hours, meet an associate, work all day, and drive back home.

On my way home, I would call home with an estimated time of arrival or Chris would call me and ask if she could go tubing when I got home. Upon getting home, I would be greeted by Chris (and of course the dogs) and sometimes a friend or two. I would see a smiling face full of glee and anticipation of the fun to come out on the lake. I would not have time to sit down and shake off the drive. I would change; jump into the speedboat, and off we went. We would tube up and down, around and around, jumping wakes of other boats or our boat.

The goal for this activity is to go fast enough to have the tube hit the wave and get "air" with the rider screaming! My goal was also to not go too fast, "Safety first" remember. We have been very fortunate through the years. A few water bumps and scrapes but no serious injuries.

Then we would head for the dock, for swimming, jumping off the dock, and just enjoying the water. Then it was time for a quick bite of dinner, and off to the pontoon and the sandbar. What fun! This would be repeated many times over the high school years and beyond.

In Michigan, the summers are way too short and the winters are way too long! Blink your eyes and it was fall and back to school for another year!

Chris's passion for horses continued in High School. She was on the equestrian team and was co-captain in her junior year and captain in her senior year. After that, she would still go and help out with the coaching.

The sophomore year was busy and uneventful. Chris loved school and did not miss a single day. There always seemed to be a lot going on, equestrian team practice and events, music events, volunteer work, 4-H meetings, riding lessons and sleepovers and of course boyfriend drama's.

Next the junior year was upon us and it was time for more freedoms. We purchased a vehicle for Chris to drive. I chose a used Ford Ranger pick-up because of its durability and long mileage record on the road, and it's full truck frame with 4-wheel drive.

We live 16 miles from town in an area that gets a fair bit of snow and 4-wheel drive seemed to be a good choice. A pick-up also fit into her equestrian lifestyle, with the ability to haul saddles, hay grain etc. An additional benefit, it has a small back seat, making it uncomfortable to haul kids around with.

One winter's day, Chris was driving and she slipped off the road into a ditch; she quickly turned on the 4-wheel drive and simply drove out! That would not have happened in a small compact car. The weather did not slow her down at all, but she did slow her speeds down when the roads were slick and snow covered.

Chris, on one of her first days with the truck, decided to go off road. I had asked her not to go off road as she was still an inexperienced driver. My intuitive thinking was on high alert one day and it directed me to her boyfriends hunting property. I waited for about 20 minutes at the entrance to the acreage and sure enough out of the brush drove Chris and her boyfriend. Chris wondered how I knew she was there, but she has become used to my intuition.

I sent her home and grounded her for an appropriate amount of time. Logic was that if she had bought the truck, paid for the insurance and repairs then it would be her decision to go off road. Since I paid for the truck then I felt comfortable with setting the rules. If you break the rules, you pay the consequences. That's life.

I still suffered from DWAS syndrome (Dad's Worry And Stress Syndrome) but the cell phone helped out. At night Chris would give me a call and let me know when she was on her way from a friends or practice. It kept the palpitations to a minimum.

One of our favorite shows is "The Mentalist" with Simon Baker. His antics are certainly at a higher level than my intuitive thinking, but it seemed on the normal side at my house. Chris had gotten used to my intuitive thinking. She had a friend staying with us for a while and her friend broke curfew. I called her to inquire where she was at and she said she was at a relative's house and I said no you are not! You are with friends, out on the deck and your breaking curfew. I have no idea how that popped into my mind, but it did. I told her to come home immediately and she did.

She asked Chris how does your dad know these things and Chris told her "Don't lie to Dad, I don't know how, but he knows".

One winter night, we had friends over at our home for dinner and the phone rang, I picked it up and said" So, you're in a ditch, where are you at?"

Chris paused and said "How do you do that?"

She was of course down the street in a ditch.

∾

I want to take a moment and discuss the pride that a parent can feel for a child. Pride in this sense is a good thing. Some parents take it too far and try to have a do-over. They try to live their lives again vicariously through their children, to the point of taking credit for their children's successes.

What I'm talking about is the enjoyment that emanates from seeing your child perform well. Yes a parent can be supportive, but they should not push kids into a sport or activity that the kids don't want to do. This is important, because resentment and a dislike for the sport or activity can result.

I'm not talking about reminding kids to practice their chosen sport, that's ok to a point, but be there for advice if asked and to help them grow and develop in their chosen activity. I felt proud of Chris's successes; I did my best to be supportive, and let her bask in her accomplishments.

In her junior year, even though there were agreed to curfews, there were some late nights. I don't think that I've caught up on my sleep yet!

There were many activities that usually meant curfew extensions; bonfires, dances, prom nights, cast parties after the play, double dating to a movie that was 45 minutes away, sleepovers, parties at our house, snipe hunting at Shelley's.

Yes I survived the lack of sleep, which was particularly tough on Saturday night, as I needed to get up by 6:00 a.m. to cantor at 8:00 a.m. service. My theory on cantoring is that all church singers receive the blessing of the angels. By that I mean that the singers sing, and the noise passes through and is enhanced by the angels. At least I hope so, that particular thought has given me courage many a time as I began singing in front of the entire congregation.

Senior Year! All hail the seniors! All Hail the Conquerors! Yes they have made it to their Senior Year! And all of the fun honors that go with it. The diploma, adulthood, an invincible feeling that you will live forever and that you have the world by the tail! Yep it's time for senior skip day, prom night, all night parties, more bon fires, homecoming game and then the hard reality that high school is almost over. There is a strange feeling of sadness, of leaving friends, and teachers behind. We know that life will change, and you can never go back to high school as a student again.

Graduation day puts a stamp of finality to the High school years. The graduation party is so much fun, and planning and work.

There will be pictures, awards, videos, family and friends. Of course food, and lots of gifts. There were gifts of money for future education, or life events. There were practical gifts and fun gifts. And at the end of the party, of course clean up. And a very significant chapter in everyone's life is closed. Where did the time go?

For many students they shift into a college mode, probably changing their career plans several times along the way. Some students move off to trade school, and learn a marketable skill. For some it means going to work, not having a skill or a degree, finding a place to fit in and earn a good wage. Some find themselves starting a family and trying to get ahead. And others join the military.

The future is not always fair. But it is an opportunity! Every day the sun comes up in the morning and the future is ahead of us. The choices we make, lead to who we are and to what we become in our lives. Then the day ends, we go to sleep, and in the morning it stars all over.

My family always chastises me because I always ask "What's the plan for today?" I believe that if you do not plan your day, you may miss something important.

Remember, "Every day is a gift; some are just more fun to open than others."

I try to pack a lot in a day that is certainly true, because I know what it feels like to not know if there will be another day!

8 COLLEGE & CHOICES

The High School years seemed to go so quickly, it was then time for Chrissy to go to College. College is a time to learn, to grow, to experiment, to make decisions and to find out who you are and for many, to change your mind multiple times on what you want to do for the rest of your life.

Some go to college because they are driven to learn for the sake of learning, some go to learn a specific skill set. Others go to college because mom and dad said that they either had to get a trade, go in the military or go to college. Others go to keep up their health insurance and to not have to pay mom and dad room and board.

College is a special time in the lives of those who choose to go and apply themselves. Socially you move from a smaller dynamic filled with cliques, rules, family connections and supervision. College, for many will be the first time that they will live in an environment where after move in day there are no rules to hold them back! As soon as the parents drive away they feel that they have instantly achieved adulthood!

Some seem to handle this new freedom very well. Some adjust to setting their own rules and set a course to succeed even with occasional stumbles along the way.

Others let the new freedoms handle them. For some, the answer to no control is out of control.

Imagine an experiment with no hypothesis. You just never know what the end result will be!

Chrissy, being human, stumbled on occasion, but she kept moving forward in the educational process. Like many, her original plan for a degree changed. She wanted to be a veterinarian, but this changed in her first year away at school.

Dear parents reading this book, it's ok for young adults to change their minds, once, twice or more until they find what they really want and are capable of doing. Remember the happiness factor in aligning what you love to do with what you will do in your career choice. It matters! Support them and guide them only if asked to do so.

I remember being there for the first day of Chrissy's kindergarten class, first grade and so on. I could not be there for the first day of college, but I was there for move in day!

∾

Move in day, Wow! Talk about episodic insanity! I mean really! Many colleges stagger their students (before they stagger themselves) by day and time of day to move in.

And of course the whole "FAM damily" has to come to move in day! There are so many people, and parents that are sobbing out of control, offering advice (at this point it won't matter) and giving out cash for carryout meals!

We packed the F-250 pick-up to the gills with stuff for the move into the dorm. We went to find a parking place and the episodic insanity was in full force! There were people everywhere!

There were cars with U-Hauls attached, car caravans, and multiple people with stuff in multiple cars and I mean a lot of STUFF! George Carlin would have been proud of all the STUFF people brought! We were directed to a parking place and given a time limit on our parking pass. Chrissy was located on the top floor of the dorm which meant taking (and waiting for) an elevator. We made multiple trips, carrying more each time that was humanly possible, but we got it all loaded into the dorm room.

Next of course after all of the physical labor, Chrissy and Carol were starving! We took off and had lunch at a great burger joint, and then Chrissy asked if we could go to Wal-Mart to pick up a few essentials. After all we moved in what else could she possibly need?

We entered Wal-Mart and the first clue was Chrissy grabbing a large shopping cart; I prefer the small carts, as you can fit less in! She picked up a lot more stuff, feminine stuff, school supply stuff, lamps, fans and of course a ladder contraption that would not fit into the shopping cart! I was not sure what the ladder would be used for, but Chrissy wanted it. We went to check out with two carts and two items that were too large to fit into either cart!

Next, we had to go back and wait in line for another time limited parking spot! We unloaded all this new stuff and there did not seem to be room for it, considering her roommate had not yet arrived with her stuff!

It was getting time for mom and dad to leave, to head up north for home. Emotions swelled up, as did the tears. It was time to go, but I did not want to leave just yet. I knew it was time to go, but I was leaving my daughter behind, to make her way on her own. And yes she was ready; I on the other hand was not.

All the students really want is for their family to get out so they can start to get settled.

"It's going to be ok, I'll be all right, and yes I will remember all you taught me!"

Then the family is gone, and it's time to negotiate with your new roommates, who gets which bed, desk. Simple things like room temperature, music or TV, volume of the noise, were all in the compromise mix.

And finally, there needs to be time limits for friends to be over, time limits for clothes on the floor, and other items that need to be settled.

Interruptions of the phone ringing, just the family calling to say they made it home safe, when really they just want to know that the student is safe.

Chrissy's roommate did not show up until 2:30 in the morning and then wanted to move in, too late to negotiate and get all of her stuff settled. This could have been accomplished over the next few days and weeks, but it did get completed by 5:00 a.m. after the move, short night!

Some families want to communicate frequently, some daily, some weekly, and some not at all. I wanted to talk twice a day at first and then just once a day. This was way too frequently. Chrissy was ok with it, she knows that dad means well, but he doesn't always get it! With time, I knew that I would be able to let go more and more.

∾

I remember the first night after move in day. The house seemed oddly quiet. I felt a deep emotion that my life as well as Chrissy's life was going to change forever, and it did.

It reminded me of a time after I moved out of my parents home, into my own home. I went back and hugged my mom and dad. We talked about how our relationship would change now that I moved out. I was now on my own, with my new wife. We shared deep emotions and thoughts about the new circumstances, and agreed that life is a series of changes, but one thing would never change, they would always be mom and dad, and I would always be their son.

Chloe, Chrissy's golden retriever seemed blue. Chloe knew that something was different, that something had changed. She would be outwardly o.k., she still was very playful, but she was unsettled and at times moped around. She missed Chrissy at every level.

She began to lick the hair off her paw; she licked and licked and licked! She looked like she had just invented an ice cream cone only it was her paw! Now when you looked at her paw, you saw skin, red from licking. It started to get infected so Chloe went off to see the veterinarian.

She was treated with an antibiotic and ointment for the infection and of course Prozac for the obsessive-compulsive behavior.

Chloe on Prozac! The therapy session went well for Chloe. She just loved the whole couch bit! After a while the hair grew back and the couch developed some ruts! It was a small price to pay for her sanity and her furry paw!

I increased my efforts to walk and have playtime with Chloe, she responded, but we still kept her on Prozac.

∽

I had attended an orientation for parents at the university, and they stated that the divorce rate for parents once they are empty nesters is 50%. I guess they have to get to know each other after 17 to 19 years of not knowing each other and some things have changed.

The orientation also addressed the fact that the students are adults now and as parents, we have no business setting any ground rules at school or in fact at home, when they come back to visit; get laundry done and ask for more money!

I understood what they are saying, but to me an adult is a fully functioning member of society.

An adult that has assimilated into a role that generates income, makes them self sufficient, autonomous and responsible for their own actions. Until then to me they are young adults.

Being young adults for a time is helpful to learn to make the big decisions. There is no rush to grow up. It seems to be true that children cannot wait to be teenagers, teenagers cannot wait to be young adults, and young adults think that they are already mature adults! They do not realize that they were not mature adults, until they become mature adults!

Of course mature adults sometimes long for the times that they were children, teenagers or young adults. They long for the times that they were without all of the bills and responsibilities. The elderly have experienced a lot in their lives. Some want to start over, but many do not. Some have regrets, and some are happy with what they have accomplished and what they intend to accomplish in their golden years. Some are not happy. Plan your life to make sure you're happy!

Episodic insanity can occur when people try to live their lives outside of their current developmental stage. Consider a teenager, trying to live as a mature adult. Some pieces of the puzzle are there, and some are missing.

Let's consider another scenario, an elderly person who is trying to live as a child. Psychiatrists call them delusional. If they are wealthy they call them eccentric!

It is critical to keep on reaching for the stars and to have dreams. Dreams are the inspiration for life.

I remember in a high school speech class, we were given a simple assignment: What is the answer to the secret of life?

That's a nice little assignment for a teenager.

I spent a lot of time contemplating this issue. Then it dawned on me that the secret to life is the question. Yes the secret of life is the process of learning and always searching for more answers. It's in the process that we learn, get excited, gain fulfillment, and that leads to the next question and on and on. It is a little confusing, and fertile ground for episodic insanity!

How difficult it was for me to let go. Caring for and watching out for Chrissy had become a very deep-seated habit. Letting go of a habit for most people can be a difficult thing to do. I had spent 18 years of keeping track of Chris as she grew up. I always tried to be there to help, and support her. Chrissy would take on new goals that she set for herself, and I would always try to garner resources to help her attain her goals.

I encouraged getting good grades in school. Chrissy is very capable of and usually attained a high grade point average. I only asked her to do her best, and to make a solid effort; if that would have occurred and the grades were not as high, I would have been accepted the result.

We have talked about her passion for horses, but it went beyond that. I fostered her interest in computers starting at a very young age and purchased new technology to get her comfortable with this tool. I provided her with educational software disguised as games to help prepare her for each grade level. She would play them during the summer and I believe it gave her a platform to build upon each year.

In High School she wanted to sing in madrigals, a competitive music group. I provided money for voice lesson for her. She did accomplish that goal, she earned a spot in madrigals, but could not attend due to a conflict with her internship at a veterinarian office and the madrigal schedule. Chrissy chose to attend the internship at the veterinarian office.

Let me be clear, all that Chrissy has accomplished in her life was due to her efforts; I just helped with resources for her to accomplish her goals!

One of her goals was to go to a major university, She did obtain some scholarships, but mainly she went on the D.A.D. Scholarship. This consists of local funding through the income deletion act of 2008. And believe me it deleted a lot of my income!

So it was time to let go, I had started the process in her freshman year, letting go a little at a time. I let go a little more each year. I felt that she was ready and ready or not the time had come. She was away at college and on her own at last! I still had a tough time with her being gone. My protective instincts still have a hold on me. Chris was living at a major university and I was not there to look out for her. I trusted her, but not the world around her.

Chrissy was not happy being away from the things she loved, her dog Chloe, her horses, her boyfriend, her home and ranch. Maybe mom and dad fit in there somewhere. I did not realize how unhappy she was until a while later, when she shared with me how blue she felt away from home! She wanted to have her vehicle on campus so she could come home on weekends. This proved to be a difficult hurdle to overcome!

The drive to pick her up was a little over two hours and then of course the drive to drop her off was a little over two hours, on a weekend that was eight hours in the car for transportation.

With the cost of fuel, I decided to take action and find a way to have her keep her vehicle with her.

We wrote to the campus police, requesting a waiver and we were told no. No never stops me, so I went on line and looked at storage sites for her to park her Reanger at during the week. None were close enough to campus, requiring a bus ride to get close to their locations. It seemed hopeless.

I then remembered that I had parked at city owned garages just off campus to go shopping or have a meal. I contacted the city garage and found an acceptable site right off campus in the shopping district.

The cost for the 24-hour access parking spot was $80.00 a month. When compared to fuel for eight hours twice a month or more, it made financial sense to obtain the parking facility.

Chrissy was able to have her pick-up with her and be able to drive home on weekends to get back to her life. I will always wonder if I would have not secured the parking for her truck if she would have adapted to university life and have learned to enjoy it. Life is like that; you make a decision, and go with it. But sometimes you look back and wonder if it was the right decision.

As with most decisions, you need to look forward, not backward. It must have been right or I would not have made it. At least I hope so.

ॐ

Life is different with Chrissy gone away to college. Life is still very busy with the horses, dogs, cats and various critters. Working the ranch is a commitment. A minimum of effort is at least twice a day, and the fact that we stall the horses at night means we spend a bit of time mucking out the stalls on a daily basis. The dogs also need exercise, care, food, water, petting and companionship. Cats can fend for themselves, but for some reason our barn cats seem to just about attack me for attention. They love to be petted, and I love the purring sound.

My career takes a lot of time, discipline and commitment. I'm a sales manager and I take my job very seriously. My objective is to exceed the company's goals and the goals of my employees. 60 to 80 hours a week. I don't mind the effort. I have the passion, the competence and the drive to continue. I truly do care for the people who I work with.

With all of that going on and my volunteer work, I still find that I miss my daughter.

I'm sure that moms and dads all over the world share this feeling when their sons and daughters go off to college, the military, missions, or to find employment and to begin their own grand adventure.

Chrissy was very good about keeping in contact. We talked at least every night to catch up on the day's events and of course so I could sing her our little song. I know the time has probably passed for the song, but I will enjoy singing it until we decide to stop.

Chloe has been doing well on her Prozac, but she seems to know when it's Friday night and Chrissy is coming home. She looks and listens for the truck to pull up.

When Chrissy walks in the door, Chloe seems to speak her excitement with a shameless display of tail wagging, a noise that is not a whimper but a gleeful exuberant and joyful sound! It lasts about five minutes and then it's time for Chrissy to say hi to Princess and the Buffalo dog. Then she says high to mom and dad afterwards.

Afterwards comes the many bags of laundry. We thought that she might be making money off of some of the kids who didn't go home that weekend by bringing their laundry home with her for mom to wash and fold and she would take multiple loads back to school on Sunday night!

∾

There are many things that you really do not think about, but you end up missing when your child moves out. All through 7th to 12th grade, Chrissy and I would study together. My favorite was science; Chrissy would quiz me to see what I remembered from my education. It's amazing how much I remembered, Chrissy was impressed too. We would discuss her history studies together and on some of the subjects I would quiz her as a tactic for learning. It was fun and a times quite challenging.

I missed doing chores at the barn together; I missed taking walks with the dogs. I even missed Chrissy's tendency to procrastinate at doing dishes, folding clothes or doing yard work. I guess I just plain missed Chrissy being home!

There were many challenges for Chrissy at college. Like many other kids coming from a small rural school, the university setting is immense.

Let's face it we have two main roads in our community. The interstate is a half hour away in any direction. Think of the movie "Doc Hollywood" with Michael J. Fox. We even have a carriage festival, not unlike the squash festival in the movie.

We don't have a movie theatre, a Wal-Mart, a Taco Bell or a bus line. We don't have 24 hour coffee shops, pharmacies or even much going on after 5:00 p.m. except on parade, fair or festival nights.

College life can go 24 hours until exhaustion occurs. And then the alarm goes off, the coffee goes in and life goes on!

There is a lot to do on a major university campus. I bought tickets for Chrissy after some prompting on her part for "Larry the Cable Guy" and various other shows and entertainers. She attended them with friends, and loved going and getting caught up in the fun of live performances. I think she really wanted to get called up on stage as happened in San Francisco when she was 5.

Chrissy did get a bus pass, but she preferred walking or riding her bike. She must have worn through a lot of shoes, because it seemed she bought a new pair every month. Maybe she just liked shopping!

She also had a meal pass. With the Vernier propensity to gain weight, this may not have been the best idea. Maybe we should have been charged by the calorie.

Chrissy would talk endlessly about the food choices at her dorm. There was Asian food, sandwiches, choices of three different entrees, burgers etc. She loved it at first, but then it began to get boring.

What is it with kids and being bored? Let's face it life at times is boring! All of this food available 24 hours, It was a growing experience. Sounded like a cruise to me!

My brother Larry always talks about his love of cruises. I just can't imagine a cruise. It must be awesome because it seems he and his family go on one every year!

The thought of being locked on a ship with 24-hour delicious food available could be an issue for me! Okay, I still have taking a cruise on my bucket list!

Chrissy also became addicted to a "Dub" sandwhich at a local restaurant. I had one with her and it was pretty good. The other college staple of course is pizza. There is cheap pizza, expensive pizza, ethnic pizza, meat lover's pizza, vegetarian pizza, bacon lettuce and tomato pizza and no cheese pizza (what's the sense?).

There is thick crust pizza, thin crust pizza, square pizza, deep-dish pizza, pizza rolls, and pizza sandwiches. There is geographic pizza, Hawaiian pizza, Southern barbeque pizza, Texas pizza (really big!), gourmet pizza, frozen pizza, homemade pizza and whole grain pizza. Chrissy would say ' hold the green peppers and anchovies!

Let's not forget about desserts, cookies, muffins, cakes, pies and especially ice cream! There is soft serve ice cream, hand dipped, freezer ice cream, vendor ice cream, Dairy Queen ®, stone cold, ice cream cones, ice cream scoops, ice cream sandwiches, ice cream dots, ice cream drumsticks, ice cream on a stick.

Don't forget about ice cream cakes and we even found a place that makes ice cream spaghetti. The ice cream includes something that looks like meatballs, but they were made of chocolate!

It must be obvious to all that when you are studying your brain burns a whole lot of glucose and calories. That's why students need to replenish with high fat high calorie foods. That's why Hagan Daz has single serving pints.

∾

Back on the home front, mom and dad paying for college is quite a draining experience. We found that we were constantly looking for ways to still have fun and not spend a lot of money. Take a look all around you, there are bargains out there if you seek them out!

We have found some real deals for our dinning pleasure. Monday nights a local restaurant features Coney dogs $1.50 each. Tuesday there's a fish dinner available for under $5.00. Wednesday is steak for $9.99 at the deluxe restaurant, or 3 tacos for 3 bucks. Thursday is karaoke and tacos for a $0.99. Friday you can hit a variety of fish fry's and Saturday and Sunday you eat at home!

We shop a bit more rather than just buying whatever we want.

We shop at dollar stores, K-Mart, Wal-Mart and Save-a-lot. We look for sales and only pay cash. We are not as adept at spending less than Clark Howard, but we are working on it!

By the way, hey Clark, how about painting your studio walls for your TV show; I understand being frugal, but really!

We backed down on satellite TV, our cell phones and landlines. We are trying to drive less, eat less and Carol is rolling her own cigarettes (Quitting would be better). We have dialed down the thermostats, the lights and some of the recreational activities.

We have found other activities that are fun and frugal. We started bowling again. On Tuesday mornings from 9:00 a.m. to 12:00 noon there is coffee and bowling, all you want of both for 5 bucks! I still love to attend the high school football games and music concerts. Also high school and community plays offer great entertainment with the bonus of supporting your community!

∾

Spring Break! What images come to mind when you think about spring break and college girls? "Girls Gone Wild DVD's"? Florida beaches with thousands of young girls all lathered up marinating in the sun for other college boys to take advantage of?

94

Do you image college kids overindulging in booze, drugs and sex? Spring Break indeed has earned a bad reputation across America. Keep in mind that most of the kids on spring break rely on funding from mom and dad. Parents of America, are we paying for the corruption of our young adults?

Chrissy's first spring break was coming up fast. I was not sure what she wanted to do. My mom called and wanted to go and visit my brother in Texas, but did not want to fly done there by herself and wondered if Christy would go with her. At 89 years old that seemed like a reasonable request. I just did not know how to approach this with Chrissy. As I pondered what to do, the phone rang and believe it or not, it was Chrissy. She was thinking about spring break and asked me if she could fly down and visit my brother Larry and his wife Ruth in Texas for spring break!

Wow, it is amazing when things out of the blue come together and make everyone happy! It is times like this when God's plan seems so apparent! I asked if she would fly down with grandma who also wanted a visit and it was agreed upon!

I called my brother and he was thrilled that both mom and Christy were coming for a visit. We worked out the date and all was set. We discussed Chrissy's visit, and it was to be a laid back time for her to get warm in the sun!

Chrissy's time in the sun was turned into an unbelievable trip, thanks to brother Larry and his wife Ruth, a very successful lawyer in Houston. It seemed that every day had something planned that was more fun than the next. I mean Chrissy had the opportunity to see what success in business and life can do for recreation, entertainment, relaxation and of course, one of her favorite pastimes shopping!

Yes Chrissy was in for true hospitability, Texas Style! They took her and grandma to a rodeo, a concert, and dining out for lunches and dinners at truly fine dining establishments. Ruth booked a fantastic Spa day for Chrissy and grandma, complete with massage and literally a head to toe makeover!

And to make sure she would never forget her spring break in Texas, Ruth took her shopping multiple times at the best shops! Her generosity made quite an impact on Chrissy.

She came away from her spring break with a clear understanding of what success can translate to in regard to lifestyle! And that was Ruth's true gift to her!

As the saying goes, it's hard to keep them down on the farm once they have seen Gay Pari!

Chrissy returned home from Texas, very grateful to Ruth and Larry. She also enjoyed spending time with Grandma, and she was a very, very happy young women!

∾

After her first year at the university, Chrissy decided not to go back for her sophomore year. Being away from the things she loved was just too difficult at this point in her life. So the following fall she attended a local community college to give her more time to decide exactly what she should chose to go into.

While online one night, she discovered a school that would give her the opportunity to do what she loves to do, work with horses. The school offers a program that earns a BS in Equestrian Studies! And the next chapter in her college career seemed to give her the drive to complete her degree, and she applied!

9 THE LITTLE MIRACLE IN GLADWIN

Early in 2008 spring had sprung, and it was time to begin getting into shape for all of the summer activities. I have noticed as the years have progressed, that each year getting into shape is a little more difficult. Keep in mind that what I mean by getting in shape is to get back to walking four miles with the dogs, swimming and bike riding. I'll never see a 32-inch waist again. At least not on me!

I usually begin the process of getting into shape with walking. This particular spring I noticed that after about 300 yards I was feeling some discomfort or pain in my hips. This seemed unusual and I felt a little out of breath. I shook it off and continued to walk. I had to stop periodically and rest before continuing. This was about April, and I remember thinking to myself, "Wow! Getting into shape this year is harder than ever!"

I continued, but did not have the same zip in my step as usual even in the spring. I made a note to do more work on the treadmill next winter, so I would not have to go through this experience again.

I continued to walk on a regular basis, even though I noticed that my energy was not quite up to par. The spring gave way to summer, and all of the activities that go

97

with the hot weather, warm evenings with longer days.

With daylight until ten o'clock in the evening, you can pack a lot of activities into a day. I love summer.

I kept noticing little things. While singing at services on Sundays I would run out of breath on long passages. This was very unusual for me. Normally I could sing paragraphs and still have a lot of reserve breathing ability. Proper breathing is critical for correct singing.

At the end of my workday, I noticed that I needed to sit on the couch and relax. I needed to take a nap before I would engage in additional activities. This was very different from my usual get home and get going on walks, boating or to the barn to bring the horses in. I attributed this to getting older. After all, even Dr. Einstein took naps during the day.

I found that I had a tougher time working at night, completing administrative tasks, coaching reports and planning activities. I just couldn't burn the candle at both ends anymore.

As usual, as the water warmed I began doing my swimming exercises. The regimen is a pretty good work out of various swimming strokes up and down the lake in front of my house. But again, this year building up to the number of repetitions was difficult to do. My breathing, which is important in swimming, was coming up short.

The symptoms kept getting worse as the summer went on. I usually cover my pontoon at the end of the day, but that became too much of a chore.

I seemed to get really tired after a couple hours of driving, and working all day. I was used to a busy schedule and long days, but not used to being this tired.

I just could not understand what was happening. I kept thinking that I was just out of shape and getting older.

∾

Humans are very adaptable; it really is amazing to look at how humans have expanded across the globe. From Eskimos surviving in the extreme cold, to the Moors whom are desert dwellers living in extreme heat. We adapt to climates, we learn, we have a big brain and thumbs!

I had a college professor, Dr. Ireland who shared an interesting theory that the reason human beings have survived may not have anything to do with our intelligence, socialization or survival skills. He suggested that according to one theory, that we simply don't taste good to animals!

Even something as simple as the aging process shows our incredible adaptability. We sleep less and eat less. As we get older we seem to get colder!

As we age we wear warmer clothes and clothes with less weight. We get more vaccinations, more doctor visits and more things either don't work as well, hurt or don't work at all!

Most of us come into this world crying, bald and with no teeth, often we leave it crying, bald and with no teeth! Many of us even wear diapers at both the beginning and the ending of our lives.

In difficult living situations we modify our behavior or try to escape with our imaginations. In extreme situations we may develop multiple personalities to be able to totally escape from a situation.

People adapt. With injuries we learn to use crutches, canes, wheel chairs, artificial limbs, new joints and in the future view we may graft new appendages. We modify, adjust, adapt, get creative and move forward. I guess that is what I did in the summer of 2008.

I traveled and spent many overnights with my job. I found that as I checked into the hotel and I brought my luggage up, it was usually about 5:30 p.m. The first thing I wanted to do was to take a short nap. This was new for me, I used to change and go out for a walk or shopping, then dinner. The nap was all I wanted to think about and all I wanted to do. I would nap until 6:15 p.m. just a short amount of time, and then I would be ok to get up and go places.

For me this was very unusual behavior. Humans are creatures of habit; my habit was long, sustained and consistent activity as I have been working to 33 years. I just hardly ever took naps. But in the spring and summer of 2008 that all changed.

Everything changed.

Cutting the grass at home used to be no big deal; I would knock it of in about an hour. But that summer, I would have to stop after about 10 minutes and catch my breath. I also noticed that my heart was pounding and I was sweating more than the effort justified. I would calm down, let things get back to normal and resume cutting.

In July it was time to stack hay up to the rafters in the hay barn. It was a hot and muggy night as it usually is, but as I stacked hay, I had to take frequent breaks. I also went outside of the barn and literally hosed myself off to cool down.

Whatever was happening to me continued to slowly march on and take away my energy, my breathing and my focus. It moved very slowly. I compensated, thought I was getting older and was just out of shape.

I guess I should have known that something was happening to me and it wasn't good. But I kept on going.

On one of my overnights, I shaved in the morning and cut myself. It just kept bleeding. I showered got dressed and it kept bleeding. I went to a breakfast meeting with associates and it kept bleeding. It bled all morning, just a little at a time, I kept putting bits of tissue paper on it to help it coagulate, but it took until lunch to stop bleeding. I guess I should have noticed that it was unusual, but I kept on going.

I was heading off to Chicago for a business review with my boss and I stopped by Michigan State University where my daughter Chris was attending school. I took her out for dinner on my way. I loved stopping in and spending time with her.

I noticed that I was getting very short of breath even though we were not parked that far from the restaurant. We ate a couple of dubs, a sandwich she loves to eat. And again on the walk back to the car, I needed to take a break from walking and I was short of breath. That was unusual, but I kept going on.

I drove to Chicago, checked into the hotel and took a nap, but this time I slept until 9:00 p.m. and woke up still tired and not hungry. Not hungry for a Vernier is a very unusual feeling. I went back to sleep and got up the next morning.

I was hungry and ate breakfast, with coffee and orange juice. I went to the branch for a business review and noticed that I was disappointed when I couldn't park close to the building.

I had to walk a little at a time and made it into work. I noticed my energy was low, and again my breathing was not normal!

I met with my boss and we began the review. I felt I was doing alright, but knew that I was tired. It was 12:00 p.m. and time for lunch.

Lunch was a short walk across the parking lot. I walked with my boss and an associate, and asked to take a couple of breaks from walking as I became short of breath. We had lunch and walked back, again taking several breaks along the way.

We sat at the table in the meeting room and my boss said that it did not look like I felt well and that he wanted me to leave early and go home. I agreed and said that I would see him in Philadelphia on Monday. He told me to skip the meeting on Monday and to go to my physician and get a check up.

So, I left for the drive home. It was a long drive of about six hours in good weather, with a stop for a bite to eat. I noticed that I was tired and so I took frequent stops to rest and to get refreshed. It was a dark and rainy night; nights like that can make it tough to see the road and be very stressful.

I remembered lots of stops to refresh myself, I felt very tired, very tired. I made it home about 11:45 p.m. I went straight to bed. That was Thursday night.

I woke up on Friday morning, still felling very tired. Chris was coming home today and it was her birthday!

I was very excited to see her and I did not want to go into the hospital ER on her birthday! Also, Friday's where I live; the physicians have a day off. So I waited for Chris to come home from Michigan State University.

2:30 p.m. Chris arrived home. I was so happy to see her. It was her birthday so she opened her presents, indeed one of her favorite things to do. But I could tell by the way she looked at me she was concerned.

"Dad, I think we need to take you to the hospital to get checked out!"

It just so happened that Carol's cousin was up for the weekend at their cottage. Carol asked her to come over. She is a Registered Nurse. She looked me over and stated that I looked jaundiced and agreed that I should go in to the hospital and get checked out. I just did not want to go on my daughter's birthday. Chris insisted and off we went on what would become the journey of my life!

Well small communities have small hospitals. As we checked in I stated that I was not sure that I should be there, but the triage nurse assured me that I needed to be there! They put me in a room, drew blood and I waited with Chris. After about an hour the physician on call came in and said that my hemoglobin was at 4. She stated that I should be either passed out on the floor or possibly dead. That caught my attention!

She said that she was going to transfuse some blood into me to raise the hemoglobin. This takes a while to drip the crimson fluid into your body, an odd feeling to see the red blood coming down the line and into your arm. Of course time kept marching on. Chris went home to sleep.

They checked my hemoglobin and it went up a little. They repeated a transfusion four more times during the night. The doctor was very concerned because it did not raise the hemoglobin very much. It should have brought it back to normal. But it did not.

Something was not right. The doctor suspected a problem with my blood. She contacted a specialist at a renowned hematology center in Detroit, Michigan. They wanted me to come down as soon as a bed was open.

At first I did not want to go. I just felt that I had a bad cold and was run down. But the physician insisted that I was in bad shape and that they could determine my diagnosis and had more in their bag of tricks to keep me going in case of any complications.

It was now the second night. My Priest visited and gave me the sacrament of "Anointing of the Sick." It all seemed like a dream or a nightmare.

While all of this was going on, family, friends, associates all began placing me on various prayer chains. I did not know the extent of the number of chains until much later. It was impressive, and I truly believe in the power of prayer!

The call came in and they had an open bed. I hoped it was open do to someone recovering. I told the physician that I would be happy to drive myself the two and a half hours to the hematology center. I was informed that I would have an ambulance take me there.

I was straddled on top of a two foot covered board, for two and half hours. The drivers were great, we discussed what exits we passed, how long they were paramedics, where they lived in the area, how the fishing was etc. It seemed to take forever, but

101

then we arrived.

We pulled up to the lobby and entered at the side entrance. No one was there to greet us, as it was two something in the morning. First we tried the basement, and they rolled me around a couple of corridors, it felt like some B movie that I was watching. Then after about 20 minutes a security guard found us and directed us to an elevator to take us to the correct floor.

Once we were on the correct floor, they rolled me into a room; a private room, thank God. I was given a private room because my immune system was so impaired that they wanted to reduce the chance of my getting an infection.

The room had an interesting smell; it was a kind of sweet bleach, with thick soapy overtones. But I was there. The nurse came in, she was very nice, and helped me get acclimated to my new room. Then it was time for sleep.

Hospitals are not conducive to sleeping, that might be why they give patients sleeping medications. But as tired as I was I went to sleep. And then morning was upon me. Time for breakfast and a parade of residents, physicians, and nurses and housekeeping staff.

Lots of residents and some lead physicians. There were teams depending on the diagnosis. My diagnosis proved to be tough to do. I was monitored, transfused, but not much else. A lead physician stated they were short of physicians and that is why it was taking a while to get me worked up.

The testing began; I had cat scans, although I never saw the cat. And an interesting test where they drill into your spine and take out some bone marrow.

As it turned out, I must have consumed a lot of calcium as a kid, they tried drilling on me for about two hours, kept breaking drills and finally gave up for the moment. They said the last time they ran into this problem was with an Olympic weight lifter. They had a nurse's aid hold my hand during the process, but after an hour, she apologized, said she couldn't take it anymore and left the room. It is a strange feeling to have drills grinding on your bones. You get the picture.

Later that day the head of the clinic, a tall, very experienced physician, came in to do the test. He found a spot that he had used in similar cases and drilled through to the bone marrow. He took out several vials. He asked me if it hurt, stated that it could be very painful. I don't understand how but at that point through Gods kindness and grace, the pain was blocked. So the exam was complete.

The results took a couple of days; they said they had a tough time with the diagnosis as there were very few of the cells they needed to find to make the diagnosis. After another day they came to me with the diagnosis.

I was suffering from aplastic anemia. There were two therapies. One was a bone marrow transplant, but I was considered a little old for that and the other, not as effective, was an oral medication.

I took out the pictures of my daughter and said I will do whatever it takes; I need to be there for Chris and to be able to watch her grow up, get through college and be there for her. They looked at the pictures and at me. I asked them if there was anything I could do and they said walk. They had a walking track around the ward and 12 trips equaled a mile. They said that patients that walk seem to do better. I began walking morning and night!

The bone marrow transplant was explained to me. I don't know who thinks up a therapy like this and of course many others therapies in this field. To me it sounded like something out of the inquisition. It would take six months to get through the transplantation and another year to fully recover if successful. They sent the transplant team to interview me and test me and decided I was an acceptable candidate.

∿

A lot of thoughts go through you mind at times like this. Dark thoughts begin creeping into your mind, deep insidious thoughts. It can be a slippery slope into depression and anxiety at times like this.

One can choose to give up or chose to fight, to live and to get better, with Gods help!

I relied on my faith in God, gave thanks for all of the wonderful things that had happened in my life and all of the gifts that God had provided, and prayed that I wanted to accomplish more with my life. I do not know how I would have handled it without faith.

Chris, Carol and friends came to visit, and I loved the time they spent with me. It felt good to have physical contact with people who I love.

The next step was to send me home, and to have my brothers and daughter tested to see if they were a good donor prospects.

There were instructions on how to sterilize the house, refrigerator, room's etc. Carol worked long days to get the house as clean as possible, Carol cleaned everything with bleach; in fact we used so much bleach it messed up our septic system! I appreciated her efforts. Also I was to keep the dogs out of my bedroom, tough for all parties involved as they had been sleeping with Carol and I since they were pups.

I could go for walks on days that were not too windy, as it was fall and lots of molds were floating around, and I was to wear a mask when I would go outside. No visitors were allowed, as they might bring in an infection.

I was so happy to go home, at times I was not sure I ever would be able to go home, so it truly was a blessing.

It was glorious to be at home even with all the restrictions. It is amazing how glorious something as simple as sitting on the couch in your own home can feel. The dogs as always were joyously happy to see me!

I remember the wonders of going for a walk with the dogs, just a half a mile on a beautiful fall day. It did seem strange to wear a mask and when the wind picked up the world did seem a little ominous, alien and dangerous. But I loved the walks.

A few days went by, and I just savored being home. A very good friend is a Reiki therapist. She asked if I wanted her to come over and give me a session. I did and she was kind enough to come.

It was my first Reiki session. She set up a large table, we said prayers and she began the therapy. She found some negative energy, a dark spot and discussed how to eliminate it. She also felt the presence of others in the room they were there to help me through this challenge.

I thanked her for the session. She suggested some prayers for me to contemplate on and she went home. It meant a lot for me that night. She is a good friend. I treasure my family and friends.

The very next day I received a phone call from the head of the clinic. He said he had good news for me. He went on to say that the he just was not comfortable with the original diagnosis. He said he would wake up at night and felt that something might have been overlooked during the review of the slides used for the diagnosis.

So he grabbed some coffee and a pathologist and they review my slides from the bone marrow biopsy for several hours. And they found something.

"I have good news!" he said. "You do not have Aplastic anemia!"

I was thrilled, choked up as a heart-pounding swell of emotions swept over me.

"What do I have?" I asked.

"Hairy Cell Leukemia," he replied.

"Leukemia, isn't that really bad to have," I asked?

"Well, between the two, we can treat Hairy Cell leukemia with a two week course of chemotherapy and some blood transfusions usually with excellent results!"

Wow, compared to a bone marrow transplant, six months in the hospital and a year for recovery. It did sound like a gift from GOD! It sounded like a miracle!

I thought of all the prayer chains, my mom's prayers, Chris's prayers, Carol's and all of my families and friends who had been praying for me. There were many people who knew me, and many that did not know me. I thought of the Reiki therapy session. I also thought of the doctor who woke up at night with something nagging at his mind that made him double check the diagnosis.

This was the "Little Miracle in Gladwin."

Yes there was still a lot to go through, but my chances for recovery were phenomenally better than with Aplastic anemia.

I thanked the doctor for his additional efforts on my behalf, he referred me to a hematologist nearer to my home and we concluded out conversation.

After our conversation I sat down on the couch; I teared up, but did not cry outwardly. I felt wave after wave of emotions that continued to well up inside me. I felt that a great pressure was lifted off of me. After catching my breath, I began first by calling Chris, then Carol, my family and close friends. Thanking them for their prayers and sharing with them the news. It became known as the "Little Miracle in Gladwin!"

Chris wanted to know more about my diagnosis, she had gone through the bone marrow testing and had read volumes on my previous diagnosis.

Our number one form of communication was texting. It's interesting that kids today text easier that they talk. Texting it seems does not seem as invasive as a phone conversation. It keeps communication shorter, gives you the ability to keep doing other things, hopefully not driving, and with on-line discussions seems to be the preferred way to communicate. I still prefer the old-fashioned telephone conversation. But I happily adapted to be able to keep in touch.

It took a couple of weeks before I met with my new doctor. I really took a liking to him. We discussed my prognosis and therapy and you could tell that his experience ran deep within him. He emanated a calmness that took hold of you and made you feel that he would do everything possible to get you through this. I have so much respect for him and the work that he does. Not every one is cured or in remission. And the flow of patients is endless. Thank God for providers like him and his staff.

My therapy consisted of a two-week course of chemotherapy and multiple weeks of monitoring and blood transfusions until things improved. By comparison of other diagnosis and therapies that may involve surgery, radiation and chemotherapy, I felt I could handle the demands, as they were easier than many other therapies. And so it began.

Chris wanted to take time off of school and come home to be with me, but fortunately after we discussed it, she stayed in school. After the first few session's I was able to drive myself to the hospital for tests, chemotherapy and transfusions. I was constantly monitoring myself for fever and any other signs of pain or unusual symptoms. By the way, chemotherapy will never be a recreational drug in the United States! There were some side effects that pop-up and needed to be dealt with, but overall I was very lucky. Some days I would get to the hospital at 8:30 a.m. and leave after 5:00 p.m.

The medical goal was to get my blood numbers as close to normal as we could. My goal was to be able to sing with the choir for Christmas Mass. I was thrilled to learn that I was not only able to sing at Christmas, but that I could have people over to the house to celebrate the holidays. And that I could go back to work in January!

I was thrilled that I could return to work, I love working. I admit that there are some tasks in my job that simply are not fun, but overall I really love my work and I'm good at it as reflected by awards, appraisals and most importantly by the people that I work with on my team.

I love seeing them be successful, and in turn that makes me successful. I have the privilege to have earned respect and many close friendships among the people I have worked with.

∾

One of the most important aspects on life is to be in a career or a job that you enjoy. Granted, not every job has a 100% enjoyment factor, that's not realistic. If you look at all of the people who hit the bars after work, or turn to alcohol or drugs before, during or after work because they simply hate what they do for a living.

Life is too short to work at something that you hate to do. It is not healthy to detest your work or to simply endure it. Find something in life that you enjoy and find a way to make a living doing it. You will have fulfillment, and joy with your career.

It is not always easy to do, but in the long run you will be healthier, happier and wealthier in ways that go far beyond the size of your home or the numbers in your savings account.

Success should be measured by truly important things. Hanging in my office is a sonnet by Ralph Waldo Emerson on the definition of success. I have shared this with many people over the years. I have tried to live my life, and to base my interactions with people on my Christian Values, the Golden Rule and the simple words that follow:

"To laugh often and much; to win the respect of intelligent people and the affection of children; to earn the appreciation of honest critics and endure the betrayal of false friends; to appreciate beauty, to find the best in others; to leave the world a bit better, whether by a healthy child, a garden patch or a redeemed social condition; to know even one life has breathed easier because you have lived. This is to have succeeded. Succeeded."

~ Ralph Waldo Emerson

If you are not in a career that you love and feel passion for, take a close look at yourself, your hobbies, and your passions. Determine what you would really love to do with your life. Then develop a plan on how to transition into your chosen career.

It may require some adjustments to your lifestyle. Granted the pay may be less, and it may not be an easy decision. Look to your inner self, to your family and friends to help you make your decision. And then take the proper actions to make sure it will work financially; you owe it to yourself to be happy!

As of today, as I'm writing this page, all is well. I'm still in remission, getting monitored regularly to keep on top of any issues that may pop up.

The reality is that there are no guarantees in life. Indeed something may come up and I could be back in the whirlwind of a new diagnosis, new therapies and an uncertain future. I give thanks to God for every day. I pray for good health and for my family and friends. I try to remember and share with everyone that I can that:

"Every day is a gift! Some are just a little more fun to open than others!"

10 FUTURE VIEW

The objective of this chapter is to look forward to the many possibilities that may occur. My brother Larry asked me, "So what's the next chapter on?"

"The future," I responded.

"The future? What do you have, a crystal ball?"

No, I do not have a crystal ball, nor do I claim to have any Nostradamus effect. I do not go into trances like Edgar Cayce did. I do enjoy some of the supermarket tabloids or "rag mags" you find at the grocery store check-out. You know, the ones that talk about alien abductions or the man that lived on cigarette sandwiches. I love the titles that claim to prophesize the future: "World's greatest prophet makes top 10 predictions," but I make no claims to be a prophet.

I was not concerned by the year 2000 supposed "meltdown" and I did not plan to spend all of my money by December 21, 2012. If the Mayan's were all that bright, they would still be here today celebrating their civilization would they not?

Whatever my skill at intuitive thinking may be, that also is not the focus of this chapter. This chapter is dedicated to the future. As we live on this earth, we remember the past, but we do not live in the past. Some of the events in our past, our actions taken or not taken, indeed impact our future. We are whom we are because of where we have been and the decisions we made.

What do we absolutely know about the future? Well, unless there is a cataclysmic event, we know that we can count on the old saw- "death and taxes." Beyond that we need to contemplate and plan for the future!

I'm very excited to see where Chris's future will lead her. Assuming that the future includes the successful launch and sales of this book, I will commit to a web site that will list the events as they roll out!

I hope that her future will include the completion of her personal goals that she has set for herself. Her passion in life has been her horses.

Chris has found a program that she was very interested in. It is a program that will give her the polish on her skills, credentials to pursue her dream of working with horses and earn her an accredited college degree. She attended the University of Findlay, in Ohio.

Due to the fact that I was no longer employed, she talked with her counselor and coaches, and ended up combining her sophomore and junior years into one. It required an immense amount of effort on her part both academically and physically, but she hunkered down and accomplished it with honors.

By comparison, her senior year was a bit more relaxing. She now holds a degree: BS in Western Equine Training. In 2012, Chris competed at the World NBHA Competition in Georgia with Blossom. What a fantastic team, she missed winning her 5D event by .049 of a second. The experience solidified her riding credentials as a finalist. Added to this Chris spent time with a million dollar barrel racer and with a high profile barrel trainer. Her future will always involve horses and she can carve out a life focused on that specific passion, she may be one of the lucky people to enjoy a life of working in a field that she loves. I hope it all comes together for her!

I remember days gone by when you would hire in with a company and for the next 20+ years your future was right there.

Today in our current economic situation, the average person will have many different jobs in their lifetime. This future view was one of the reasons that portability with 401K and retirement accounts became so important. Likewise, the same portability with health insurance is such a key issue. With the Affordable Healthcare Act or Obamacare only a couple of years old, time will tell if this was the right answer. A single payer system may be in our future.

Again, the human ability is to adapt, to be retrained, refreshed, and reenergized by taking on a new career. The challenge in the past to making these changes has been the loss of income when making a significant job change. These challenges will continue!

The future view for Chris, and many other young people, may include several different careers or positions. The future social structure of the economy looks to increase the spread between high paying jobs and low paying jobs. America is still, indeed, the land of unlimited possibilities: anyone with the right idea, at the right time, can generate significant wealth. The key is that the US economy has been shifting from a manufacturing base to a high technology and service base. Sadly the middle class seems to be shrinking.

In Chris's plan, like so many of her girlfriends, is to at some point to get married. So, her spouse will also need to keep marketable skills for the future!

Living in central Michigan has many advantages. Michigan, celebrates the four seasons:

• Planting, fishing & hunting season.

• Boating, fishing & hunting season.

• Harvesting, fishing & hunting season.

 • Snowmobiling, fishing & hunting season.

We do have less than a booming economy and jobs are scarce. We are quickly becoming a state where the population is either retired, unemployed, or on welfare.

Chris's future view and possible changing career choices will require a lot of flexibility! Partnering with her future spouse financially and emotionally for the uncertainties of the new economy seems like a tall order. I'm confident that she is up to the challenge.

I know at some point in the future, it will be Chris's time to get married and move out on a permanent basis. Believe it or not, as long as it happens when it is supposed to, she will be in her career, he will be in his career, they will be prepared emotionally and financially to take this important step in their lives, I will celebrate her wedding.

I know some couples that married very early in their lives; went through the tough times and made it, but it is becoming more and more unusual.

We live in a disposable society. We live in a time that items are almost as expensive to purchase a new appliance as it is to hire someone to come out and fix your old appliance.

And why is it that everything that is sold these days want you to purchase an extended warranty? It does not seem to matter if you buy a car, an appliance, or a video game; someone is trying to sell you an extended warranty. After I have done the research, talked to the salesperson who passionately insists that this is the most reliable unit on the market, I make a decision that I want to purchase the item. I'm then asked if I want to buy "peace of mind" for the next five years by adding in a warranty.

I just don't get it! They want me to spend $5.00 for a warranty on a $29.00 video game! Or $200 on the warranty for the washer and dryer! Or $1200 for an extended warranty on a new vehicle! Please include the warranty in your pricing. I mean, who would not want a product that has a warranty?

Well, in marriage, there is no extended warranty! So, it just makes good sense to try to line up everything you can to give you the best chance of having a happy long-term commitment!

Today, a marriage needs both parties to be in productive careers. Both partners need to earn a good income just in case one loses a job, the other can cover. Insurances are important: health, life, auto, home, etc. Also, why is it called life insurance? Shouldn't it be called death insurance?

My advice to young people planning to get married is to do it up right. After all, you only get married two or three times in your life, so have it your way! (Is that an ad slogan?)

The divorce rate in America for first time marriages is 34%, second and third marriage's are even higher! I could not find the information on fourth marriages; maybe its three strikes and you're out!

Really, the goal in marriage is to get betrothed once, for the rest of your life! Unfortunately, it does not always work out that way! In my family, on both sides, my grandparents were divorced and my brothers were divorced. They all enjoyed a happier life. So, I guess it all evens out.

On the positive side, at least half of the people that get married once stay married! For better or worse!

One sure thing about the future is that as time marches on, we get older. It sure beats the alternative, or at least it must because, as humans, it seems our goal is to put off the inevitable for as long as possible. Keep in mind that "life is a temporary inconvenience!" We are just visitors here on earth. That's ok, it is all part of the God's grand design!

Humans have long sought ways of extending life. Think of the fountain of youth; it must be somewhere in Florida because there are so many elderly people who move there and live long lives there!

The life expectancy in the US is 78.74 years. Canada is 81.24 years. It must be the socialized medicine, right? By the way, don't live in Chad, where life expectancy is only 49.81 years!

Extending life is a billion dollar industry! There are life extension vitamins, cryonics (like the Guinea pig in a really cold freezer!), calorie restriction (it didn't work for weight loss either), the Life Extension Center in North Carolina, focusing on nutrition and super foods to fight off disease (new products to sell to us!) and of course hints from Oprah's Dr. Oz! (Fitting name don't you think?).

Welcome to the "Land of Dr. Oz", where you do not have to grow old! (Didn't Dr. Kevorkian come up with a plan on not to get any older?)

How do you recognize the fact that you are getting older? Well one sure sign is when you catch yourself screaming at your kids to turn down the volume on their surround sound system. It's interesting that many people lose their hearing as they age and, if that is true, why do older people always yell at their kids to turn down the volume?

Another sure sign is when you get together with friends. You don't talk about the newest music groups, coming attractions for live concerts, or the hippest clothing style. In fact, you begin to talk about your medical problems. You compare notes as to the medications you are taking for a myriad of maladies that may come with the gift of aging. As age increases, believe it or not, a discussion about bowel functions can occur.

Remember the old saying: "An ounce of prevention is worth a pound of cure."

Age of course is not just a human condition. I look back at all of the dogs that I have had the privilege of sharing my life with.

There was Spotty, a Springer Spaniel; Monique, a rescue mixed breed and, of course Penny, Snowy, Buffalo, Princess, Chloe and now Nugget, our newest rescue dog. I introduced you to most of them earlier in the book and I hope you understand the love, fun, and companionship that our dogs have enriched our lives with. We have loved them all.

I wish dogs had a longer life span, but I guess in God's wisdom, we learn many lessons from our pets. We learn how to live in the moment and always be ready to play. We learn to live with illness, at times to ignore pain, and make the best of it. They show us how to love unconditionally and yes even how to age and to die.

Of course, one of my associates bought a parrot, with a lifespan of 75 years! He had to make arrangements in his will to take care of Polly after his demise. So I guess we do have options on choosing pet life spans.

The Woof N Whinny ranch: recent name change to CV Performance Horses, will hopefully have a long lifespan, introducing many people to the love of horseback riding. When Chris returned from college and her sabbaticals out west, she opened her lesson business to help people achieve their riding goals. This was one of our visions for purchasing the property.

One of our goals will be to add a year-round indoor riding arena and have Chris build her life at the ranch. She is on her way!

When we made the move to the country, my wife Carol said that it was her last move. I can understand her concerns. We had moved, at that point, five times in our marriage! Packing and unpacking is an arduous task.

I must confess that while I do not enjoy the planning, preparation, and the physical moving, I do enjoy the process of looking for a new home, envisioning what it will be like to live there, making new friends and actually being in a new living situation. If this is Carol's last move, it just might be my last move. Only the future holds the answer.

When it comes to adding more animals to the Vernier family, it may be time to slow down on that account. I believe that we will always have at least two dogs, because in my experience, two dogs are great companions for each other.

Two dogs play together, learn from each other and just seem to be happier. I'm not suggesting that there are never any issues between the pair, there definitely is, but we do try to teach them to share, to take turns, and to keep a healthy energy in our pack. (Cesar Milan, the Dog Whisperer, would be proud!)

Note that I talk about two dogs. I believe God gave us two hands, so we should stay with two dogs because you can only pet two at a time. I know you can pet more dogs if you juggle the petting and we have had more than two in our pack, but two is my preference. When growing up, Chris always wanted 101 dogs. Guess who would be picking up the puppy presents?

I truly hope our future includes having and caring for the horses. As previously described, they are a lot of work, but it seems therapeutic in a way. There are many examples of how working on a horse ranch benefits troubled teens, children with special needs and people in other circumstances.

I think that after doing chores and putting the horses in for the night, you feel a sense of accomplishment and meaningful purpose that is often lacking in our modern society. It gives me a grounded sense of peace in my life. After the work is done and the horses are fed, I enjoy brushing them or just stroking them, feeling the muscles, the hair, the calmness, and the overall sense of being connected to these powerful animals.

I also love the beautiful sunsets. I look at the sky as God's canvas. God creates masterpieces daily! The colors in his palette are endless. Even the grey days seem to come alive toward evening. The canvas is constantly changing and so are we. I really enjoy the red sunsets. They seem to glow and bathe everything in their warmth. It sometimes feels like I'm living in a "Terry Redlin" painting!

Lake living has been a dream realized for the last 25 years. First we lived here on weekends as a summer home and then as our permanent residence. I still love the water! I owned a boat before I owned my first car. I love to swim. I love to hear the sound of water as it crashes and rolls into the shore! The sound is so relaxing, so grounding. It may be the weightless feeling that I get when floating on the water. Or maybe it is the fact that we are made mostly of water. I know that living on the water will not last forever, nothing does. So I plan to enjoy each and every day!

As for the future, in regard to my medical challenge, I'm being monitored on a regular basis. There is hope that remission may be 20 years to life. (Sounds a little like a sentence in a criminal trial.) Anything can happen; there is no guarantee. I will continue to hope for the best and the future will unfold its secrets over time. I thank God every day for the remission and pray that this blessing of good health will continue. This experience has changed and enhanced my philosophy of life!

I have a new philosophy of learning to love and live each and every day to its fullest. It is not always easy to do; issues pop-up that take our minds away from the beauty that God surrounds us with. The little things, like the hug of a child, the greeting from a dog, the taste of a cool drink of water on a hot day, or a hot drink on a cold day! The little things have become more enjoyable.

I treasure the feeling of relaxation when I get home and have a chance to sit down on my favorite chair or sink into my comfortable couch. I love the exhilaration of taking a warm shower, a leisurely walk around the neighborhood with the dogs, and sitting down to read a good book.

I enjoy having the ability to pick up the phone and dial a friend or a loved one just to say hi!

I love a sunset, a sunrise, a rainy day, a snowy day, a foggy day, or a bright blue-sky day. Twilight is a particularly relaxing time of the day for me. When the moon and the stars come out and the nighttime sky takes on a bejeweled look, sparkling and twinkling all around us, I know God has created a world of infinite beauty! The more you look for and recognize the little things, the more depth the tapestry of life seems to take on.

Nothing is more valuable than your family and friends. Their support, prayers, and friendship helped sustain me through the dark days. You never forget the people who are truly there for you and don't forget to be there for them! We all have our times of need.

My mom passed away on her 94th birthday! Wow! How awesome is that? I often reflect on my years growing up at home, going to visit her when I had moved out on my own, staying overnight at her apartment to spend some time with her. Most of her life she was blessed with good health, living on her own until the last five years, then she lived with my brother Larry for a time and then with my family for the last year and a half. My mom is certainly destined for sainthood, as many mothers are. She had to put up with three boys growing up together.

She had also worked fulltime with my dad as a salesperson in Detroit. I remember she began working when I entered the 7th grade. I remember having mixed feelings about it at the time.

I would get home after school around 3:30 pm. It was a nice family neighborhood with good neighbors for support on both sides of our modest bungalow. Mom and

Dad would be home by 6:00 p.m. Money was tight, so it had to be done; Mom had to go to work because the family needed the income.

I will never forget how, after dark, my home took on a life of its own. The darkness seemed sinister and filled with scary things.

There was the creaking of the rafters, the sounds of the hot water heater, or furnace turning on.

If you have watched the movie "Home Alone," there is a scene that reminds me of my own situation growing up. Kevin McCallister became comfortable after going in the basement and facing his fears! But, unlike the movie, I remember remaining scared. Toward evening, when it became dark outside and I was home alone, I would take out a large butcher knife and wait at the kitchen table until I saw the lights of my dad's car turn in the driveway. I felt a great sense of relief when my parents arrived home. The perceived danger was over. I would quickly put the knife away and go sit in front of the TV, as if I was very comfortable. I just could not let them know how scared I was because I had overheard them discussing how we needed the money that my mom made to keep up with the bills.

That's how kids are at times; trying to do the right thing or at least the right thing in their minds. Looking back, I'm sure if I would have told them how scared I was, they would have made arrangements with a neighbor to keep me at their house until Mom and Dad would be home.

My concern was that Mom needed to work and I was not going to be the reason that she could not work. It all worked out in the end. I became more comfortable over time and to this day I'm comfortable when I'm alone!

Mom living to 94 was such a beautiful gift. We talk now every day through faith. Yesterday I told her how much I wished that I could pick up the phone and talk to her. I told her how wonderful that made me feel. I wish I could pick up the phone today and call my Dad and my brother Larry also! The loss of my dad and Larry made me feel alone again; I would not see the headlights pull up in the driveway. I was used to talking with my dad daily, asking for his advice and guidance. I miss his warmth, his humor, and his friendship. Likewise I would call Larry every day just to keep up on the latest events and funny stories.

I remember when my mom was in her 70's and I told her that she would make it to her 90's and she did not believe me! I'm just thrilled to have the chance to spend time with her. That is really how the future can surprise you. Mom never thought she would make it past the year 2000. Now, we celebrate each new birthday as if they were still with us. Mom passed at 94 years of age.

Take time each day and share your thoughts with your family and friends. Take a time out each day, 15 minutes or so, and spend some time thinking about where your life is going. Have you stayed grounded in who you are? Ask yourself if you are on the right path to accomplish your goals. If you do not take the time to get your bearings, you might drift off course.

What a time we are living through. I think back during my life to the Cuban Missile Crisis, the nuclear war threat, the Kennedy and MLK assassinations, the Vietnam War, atrocities in Cambodia, the Bosnia-war atrocities, the Gulf War, September 11th, the Darfur atrocities, the Iraq War, the War in Afghanistan! Today there are the terror alerts, ISIS, the tsunami in Indonesia, the earthquake in Haiti, Hurricane Katrina, the Gulf-deep horizon oil spill, Hurricanes, Asteroids, and pandemics. It would take a litany of books to list all of the human tragedies, natural disasters, plagues, and starvations. Let's not forget global warming- oops, I mean "climate change."

And what about conspiracy theories? It seems that our government can't make toilets that flush in our homes, but they can use the HAARP instrument to control the weather or even cause earthquakes WOW!

And what about Jesse Ventura's show on various conspiracies such as 9/11 or 2012? Again our government can't seem to keep the economy running smoothly, but it seems to be accused of controlling a lot of other very complicated stuff!

Is the world truly spinning out of control? What will the future bring? And what effect should this have on us as individuals and what actions should moms and dads raising a family take to protect their future? Well, in regards to spinning out of control, it is totally out of our control and always has been, so hang on for the ride!

Natural disasters are a real threat. All we can do is keep an eye on the news and have appropriate supplies for our geographic area. A tsunami in central Michigan, or a hurricane, is probably not a real threat. However, a power outage due to an ice storm, electrical storm, tornado, or high winds is something to prepare for.

A terrorist attack is also, unfortunately, a possibility, but what type of attack? How should you prepare? I don't know that we truly can prepare.

It would be great to have a crystal ball!

Remember worry and anxiety can shut you down. The key is to understand the issues and threats as best you can and continue to live your life. Worry and anxiety will not help any situation. Preparedness and knowing what action to take and when to take action will get you through many situations.

If you feel a heart attack or stroke symptom, don't worry about what might happen, take action and get medical help! Act fast. Time lost is muscle loss or brain loss, as the saying goes.

During business travels, on several occasions, I traveled with a colleague and a friend. We visited some of the finest emergency rooms around the country. One specific situation came up in Arizona. We were at a meeting an upscale resort. It was hot during the day and cool at night. My friend went into a rapid heart rate, flushing, sweating, and fainting attacks. As his friend, I was asked to accompany him to the ER via the ambulance. It was tense indeed; his heart rate would speed up, get irregular, and then slow down. The paramedics were concerned. When we arrived at the E.R., they took him in immediately.

I was in the waiting room and another company representative showed up and asked how he was doing. I explained about his heart rate and irregularities and that I was waiting to hear more. He looked glum and downright morbid.

He stated, "Well let's call his wife and let her know what was happening."

It was 11:00 p.m. our time and 1:00 a.m. where his wife lived. I told him that was not a good idea until we found out what the situation in fact was. He got hot and told me I was an idiot and that we should call his wife.

Since he did not have the phone number and I did, I controlled the situation and said that we needed to wait. So we waited. About two hours later the physician came out and talked to us. All symptoms had stopped and my friend was back to normal. They did not know what happened, but they wanted to keep him a little longer for observation. They thought that when he drank a cold soda pop too quickly, it affected his vagus nerve and that triggered the rapid heartbeat. He told us that we could go see him and we did.

Upon learning that our mutual associate wanted to contact his wife and scare the hell out of her, he told the gentleman to leave his room as he did not want to look at anyone who had the judgment of a hemorrhoid or something like that. He then told me that I had done the right thing, to wait until we knew something.

He was released and we went back and attended our meetings. It gave us something to talk about, although we were a little tired from being up all night.

A year later, at another meeting at another upscale resort in Colorado, it was about 1:00 a.m. and the phone rang.

It was my friend and he shakily said "Hey Joel, I'm having another attack, please come to my room."

I replied, "Ok, no problem, take a deep breath and try to relax. I will get an ambulance on the way and be in your room in five minutes."

It would have been quicker, but I needed to get dressed.

I quickly entered his room and he, indeed, was not looking too good. The paramedics came in, took his vitals, and we were off and running to another ER in another city.

There was a blowing snowstorm, not a lot of traffic on the road, but it took us about an hour to get there. Since this was a trip we had taken together several times before, I knew the gig. On the way to the ER I would watch and listen to his heart rate, rapid and irregular. We arrived at the ER about 2:30 a.m. and off he went to be evaluated.

A couple of hours went by, and the physician came out to give me an update. As usual, he was back to normal and they wanted to keep an eye on him for a couple of hours, which they did, and then released him about 9:00 a.m.

As we were driving back, my friend told me how much he appreciated how I always handled a crisis. I was calm, took charge, and helped him to relax and remain calm himself in tough situations.

Remember, don't worry and don't let anxiety shut you down. Take action and work through the situation!

Each time after our adventures in ER-land, he would go home and get a medical workup to no avail. But this time, with a new physician on the case, they found the cause of his misery. It turned out to be "Graves Syndrome," a thyroid issue that was easily treated with appropriate medication.

I wanted to share this story, because it is a great example of keeping your wits about you in an emergency situation. The future needs to play out; positive things can happen! My friend has not had an incident in over 20 years since he was diagnosed and treated.

Whatever the future will be, embrace the changes, learn to adapt, accept and make the best of the changes that will indeed occur. Because as we age, you can count on changes to occur in our health, our families, our finances, and everything that touches the tapestry of our lives!

What is the tapestry of one's life? Envision a finely woven tapestry. Every fiber is interconnected and dependent upon the next fiber. When you press down with your finger on one spot, it resonates through the entire tapestry.

Think of it this way. A young man looks at a beautiful woman. He may fantasize about her, not thinking past the moment of his fantasy. He is not just looking at a beautiful woman. He is looking at a complex human being, he is glancing at a moment in time, how she appears on her tapestry. He needs to look beyond that to the entire tapestry. She has a car and a home decorated in her personal style. She may have children or a relationship. She has dreams about her future and experiences from her past. There may be complications, inter-related with his life's tapestry.

I remember sharing this concept with a friend. He shared with me that he wished he understood this concept when he was younger. It may have simplified his life and he may not have indulged in as many one-night-stands.

As I'm writing this book, I have some truly difficult news. Buffalo, now 15 years old, has been suffering from a fatty tumor on her rear right leg. It is getting to be that difficult time in a dog owner's life that a decision to put her down needs to be made. I know the dog owners reading this book understand our emotions. I have seen other writings that have labored to express this critical moment. I wrote this prayer to express my feelings. I hope that the prayer may help others during this time.

Our Dogs Prayer

"I know you love me. I know because through all of the years we have lived together, you have treated me with gentleness, kindness and you have taken care of all of my needs. I remember when I first came to you as a puppy, you were house training me, and when I made a mistake, you did not hit me, you simply took me outside and praised me when I did well.

I have never felt the harshness of being hit, only the loving touch from your hand. I have always greeted you with excitement and love when you would come home, for I knew that you would take the time to play with me, to pet me and to take me for the walks that I love. You always made sure that I would have good food to eat and plenty of fresh water to drink.

Our years together have been wonderful. My life has been full of happiness and joy! I know that I have truly earned my rightful place as a member of our pack, our family. I'm proud to have shared my life with you.

I know that you understand that I'm hurting, that the ravages of disease and time, have taken away my joy of living. I know that you will do the right thing, at the right time, so that I will not suffer. I do not understand why I cannot do the things I love to do anymore.

Thank you for your kindness, once again, I place my life, my trust, and my love in you, my owner, my friend and my reason for living. I know it is time for you to help me with one more act of kindness. I'm ready to go, so I will suffer no more. Remember me, and remember that you have all my love forever!"

Life, Laughter and a Little Miracle!

We live and we die, the question is why?

What is the answer to the question of life? The answer is in the journey! The search for the answer, the learning, the striving, and the passion is what human-kind does best! We have put men on the moon, mapped the human genome, split the atom, and developed many treatments for the sick. We must continue to reach for the stars, to dream of the ultimate cures, and to finally find peace within the human family! Be sure you do not wish your life away, wishing to be 21, wishing to be graduated from high school, or college. Wishing to be married, or divorced. Wishing to be retired. Live every day to the fullest! Enjoy every day; make accommodations for yourself and others when the toll of years or disease takes something away. Live every day with your heart full of love! Smile to all that you meet; keep yourself right with family and with God. Always do the right thing!

"Remember, every day is a gift, some are just a little more fun to open than others!"

~ Joel Vernier

Thank you for taking time out of your busy life to read this book. I hope you found it worthwhile. I hope that you had some laughs, some teaching moments, and enjoyed the stories in this book.

May God bless you, and may your life be lived!

Made in the USA
Lexington, KY
05 February 2017